STRANGE TALES

— of the —

SOUTH WEST

Ronnie Hoyle

BOSSINEY BOOKS

First published in 1993 by Bossiney Books, St Teath, Bodmin, Cornwall.

Typeset and printed by Penwell Ltd, Callington, Cornwall.

ISBN 0948158 86 7

ACKNOWLEDGEMENTS
Front cover photography: ROY WESTLAKE
Front cover design: MAGGIE GINGER
Back cover photography: MARYLOU NORTH
Other photographs: RAY BISHOP; MICHAEL DEERING;
                    ROY WESTLAKE
Drawings: SARAH TOWNROW

'When I set out for Lyonnese,
A hundred miles away …

Thomas Hardy 1840-1928

About the Author

RONNIE HOYLE *is currently Chief Sub-Editor of the Western Morning News, and formerly their Literary Editor as well. During this period of dual roles he wrote such a prodigious number of reviews that he worked under six pen names (one of them was Annabel Amber!)*

A journalist since he left school in Sussex, he has been editor of two weekly newspapers, run his own newspaper in Cornwall (on two occasions) and is also associated with the North Cornwall Advertiser.

He has been writing since the age of 12 – 'the butler did it in my first story!' – when he knew what his future would be. Although he now designs a daily newspaper, he still finds time to interest himself in local history and has published two books on the history of Wadebridge.

An avid book collector (he ran his own second-hand bookshop at one time) he also writes poetry which has been published in several anthologies.

About the Artist

SARAH TOWNROW *is someone to watch out for in the future. Her name may be relatively unknown at the moment but her work shows exceptional talent, particularly her illustrations of animals, and she is destined for greater things.*

Just 21, she divides her time between her current work in Germany where she is a bookseller, and her parents' home at St Issey. She began her real interest in art at an early age and her parents, recognising her talents, engaged a special tutor for her.

Passionately interested in horses, she is also a photographic model and an amateur actress, and before taking up her present occupation ran her own windsurfing centre at Padstow. She also writes poetry.

At present, Sarah is working on a commission to illustrate a series of children's books for an American publisher.

Ronnie and Sarah are both members of the Camhayle Theatre Club at Wadebridge, where the idea of collaborating on this book was born.

Ronnie Hoyle

Sarah Townrow

CREATURES OF THE DEEP

DOWN in the depths of the seas around the Westcountry lurk monsters – those beasties of the deep which seem to be closely related to Nessie of Loch Ness. And just like their timorous cousin they seem to be particularly shy.

But now and again they raise their heads – and sometimes part of their body – above the waves to send chilly shivers down the spines of anyone who spots them.

Although it seems they have been relatively reluctant to put in an appearance for the benefit of man, they have been reported down through the centuries.

In the South West in the 1930s there was a plague of the beasts from the deep, the first authenticated report of a 'sea monster' coming on July 4, 1934, from the *Western Morning News*.

According to the report, the monster was about 10 foot long and six inches thick and was spotted near Tregantle in Whitsand Bay. The beast swam with an undulating motion, and its head was shaped like that of a snake, a description which fits many other monster sightings, not just in the Westcountry but all over the world.

Making the report to the newspaper was a Mr E.R. Gunn, of Craigmore Avenue, Plymouth, who said he was one of a party of four on the beach. 'We were sitting on the beach between Tregantle and Freathy after a swim. We saw what appeared to be a log in the water about 50 yards away. It was a black object, and then started to move, and we noticed that it was swimming towards the shore. As it passed us, we saw it quite distinctly.

BENEATH THE WAVES ... 'in the depths of the seas around the Westcountry lurk monsters ...'

The creature was not swimming like a fish, but more like a caterpillar crawls. I should think it was 10 feet long at the least.

'There were about three arches as it swam, and the tail seemed to be pointed like a snake's. It did not remind us in any way of a fish, and it was certainly not an eel. When I ran over the rocks to get a better view of it, it swam into a narrow channel only a few feet from where I was standing. It seemed to slither over the rocks and then got back into the sea again.

'I then saw that it was of a brownish-red colour, and possessed

7

no fins at all. The thing was more like a boa-constrictor, although it appeared to be in its natural element in the sea. If I had had a camera, I could easily have taken a picture of it when it was near me.'

Mr Gunn and his companion, a Mr R.E. Swiss, of Caradon, Beacon Park, Plymouth, then lost sight of the creature, but reported the incident to the Marine Biological Laboratory in the city, where scientists advanced a theory that it might have been a snake which had slithered overboard from one of the liners which frequented the port at that time.

But Mr Gunn was unconvinced by the explanation, claiming that the creature was in no way distressed at being in the sea and had even gone back into the water after coming ashore. It seemed, he said, to be swimming in a natural way.

No one, of course, knows how long these creatures live, the distance they travel or even their growth rate, but the next time a snake-like monster appeared was on May 3, 1935, at Port Isaac where it was spotted by four local people.

Lazily gliding around in a smooth sea off the Cornish north coast was what was described as: 'a monstrous glossy black creature, with long goose-like neck, a humped back, and a tremendous tail.' People who saw the creature told the newspaper they reckoned it was the second Loch Ness Monster, and had been seen on three separate occasions.

In a rather melodramatic way, the reporter set the scene: 'On Wednesday morning, a young guest-house proprietress was sitting on top of the cliffs of Port Isaac looking out to sea. Like people do on a sunny morning, she was thinking of nothing in particular when she saw a huge black monster gliding over the glistening blue sea. About one-and-a-half hours later another woman was looking out over the charming bay of Port Isaac when she saw what appeared to be a black boat. Not long afterwards a postman was delivering his letters, still a little further up the coast, when he saw that appeared to be a monster from out of a story book. It was smoothly cutting through the calm waters like a yacht at the foot of the cliff directly below him.' The report then went on to give Mr S. J. Honey, the postman of

Tintagel Terrace, Port Isaac, nearly a column of space to explain what he had seen …

'I was delivering my letters at Castle Rock, and was standing at the door of Miss Edith Donnithorne's house, when I looked down to the sea and then exclaimed: "There is a Loch Ness Monster!" Miss Donnithorne looked too and exclaimed: "So it is!" and ran for her field glasses. I saw a monstrous thing. It had a big head, just like a seal's, a goose-like neck, which must have been standing at least four feet out of the water, and there was a huge hump on its back resembling a big barrel. Floating behind on the surface of the water was a tremendous tail, tapering to a point.

'The creature was between 50ft and 40ft in length. From the edge of Castle Rock one could have jumped on to its back. It was going along smoothly, just like a yacht, heading for Port Gaverne, and unfortunately going away from me. Then it suddenly sank. There was no wash or dive, it just went down flat. I was watching it for quite five minutes, and in the beautifully clear light, I could see the sun shining on its glossy black body.'

Any suggestion that Mr Honey might have been imagining things was ruled out – after all, he was the honorary secretary of the Port Isaac British Legion and 'he was emphatic that he was a teetotaller.'

And just like many people since, who have declared that they have seen creatures from the deep, he was ridiculed by his friends and neighbours in the fishing port.

But when other people came forward and said they too had seen the monster, doubts began to be dispelled, although the stolid fishermen of the port still remained rather sceptical.

Owner of the Tre-Pol-Pen Guest House in the village, Mrs F. E. South said: 'I was sitting on top of the cliff about 11 o'clock on Wednesday morning, between Port Quin and Port Isaac, when I saw what I thought to be a very strange boat. It was a funny shape and extremely black, but I do not think there were many boats out from Port Quin, and thought it rather unusual. Then I thought no more about it until I saw Mr Honey in the afternoon. The thing was about a quarter-of-a-mile from where

HIDDEN BAY … Cadgwith Cove from a drawing by C Napier Hemy.

I was sitting and was travelling towards Port Isaac.'

Miss Donnithorne, of the Castle Rock View hotel, also told her story, backing up Mr Honey and added she thought the creature was going to clamber out on to the rocks where the seagulls had taken off in screaming fright.

'I am certain it was not a porpoise or a seal,' she said. 'It was a huge black monster, and glided smoothly towards the rocks. It seemed to know where it wanted to go, and maintained the same speed. It had no fins, which makes me think it was not a shark, and it was not the shape of a whale. I waited half-an-hour after it had disappeared, but did not see it again. It was a most frightening thing. I had never seen such a creature before, although I was born in Port Isaac.'

A Mrs Borne, of Mount Pleasant, Port Isaac reported the incident slightly differently – she thought she had seen a sinking boat, and did not bother to report it to the coastguard! It seemed, she said, like a crabbing boat which was half submerged with a man standing at one end!

The Black Beast of Port Isaac rapidly became the talk of the area, and not just in the local hostelries. The next day, it was still headline news:

'As they drifted over the calm Atlantic Ocean off North Cornwall yesterday, Port Isaac fishermen sought not only shellfish, but also a "glossy black creature, which has a long goose-like neck, a humped back, and a tremendous tail," but it was not to be seen,' reported the newspaper. 'Port Isaac folk yesterday discussed the curious creature, and whether it was a second Loch Ness monster or whether the first monster had wandered away from Loch Ness. They wondered, too, if Port Isaac would have a monster of its own.'

Just at the beginning of the holiday season, it would have been the perfect draw for visitors if the monster had put in regular appearances off the North Cornwall Coast, but the Black Beast of Port Isaac simply vanished from whence it had come. 'It was obviously making its way up the coast,' continued the newspaper report. 'It might now be off the coast of North Devon. It might have glided past Boscastle and Bude and might make a call at Westward Ho! or Ilfracombe, or leave the deep sea for some secluded river.'

In fact, it seemed it did no such thing – but turned around again and went back the way it had come, right around Land's End to the South Coast of Devon.

The journey, however, was to take several days. Officials at the

MYSTERIOUS SEAS … The Lizard lights by night from a C Napier Hemy drawing.

Plymouth-based Marine Biological Laboratory were passing the monster off as a basking shark or thresher shark. 'Basking sharks are frequently mistaken for sea monsters,' the newspaper was told. 'In this case, probably two were together and the tail fin of one of them sticking above the water might give the impression of a long neck. They are frequently met with off the Cornish coast and are quite harmless. It may also have been a thresher shark, although they are more rarely met with. This shark has a long tail, which in this case might tally with the "monstrous tail". It is, of course, impossible to tell without having seen the thing and thereby gaining a more or less accurate impression of what it looked like.'

Basking sharks in British waters, especially around the warmer seas of the Westcountry, have been seen quite frequently, and they can go up to 40ft in length, but the 'monster of the deep' seen disporting itself near Plymouth on May 18, 1935, was no shark – it had, said Mr W.R. Lavers, of Stoke House, close to Stoke Beach, Revelstoke, where he saw the beast, "a head like a calf".

He first spotted the creature when it was about 400 yards off the beach. It disappeared and then re-emerged a few minutes later some 25 yards out from the beach. 'One could see through glasses that its head seemed like that of a calf. It had a large body, and I should say it was over 7ft long. It came up every three or four minutes to breathe and disappeared as if looking for food,' said Mr Lavers, an amateur naturalist and the manager of the Co-operative tearooms in the city.

One of the party on the beach said when they shouted at it, it turned towards them and as they continued it came closer to the rocks and 'was so near that we were able to see its nostrils.' It had, he said, a 'tremendous back' and although they were unable to see much of its body below the waterline the back itself had 'a scaly appearance, and looked something like that of a whale.'

The beastie obviously took a dislike to being shouted at, and set off again. Its next appearance was in the fast-flowing waters of the River Gannel at Newquay in June where it was seen on several occasions. 'Singular features of the creature which has visited Newquay are that on each occasion it has followed practically the same route and procedure, that each time it has invaded the winding river the water has been rough, and the tide high. It has been plainly seen by at least three people, and each has given the same description, and is convinced that it is not a shark, seal, or any common inhabitant of the sea,' reported the *Western Morning News*.

First to spot the animal was Mr R.H. Northey, owner of the Fern Pit Tea Room at Pentire, who claimed he was with his brother-in-law, Mr S. Morcom, in the gardens above the River Gannel when they saw a 25ft monster gliding up the river with the tide. It swam some 400 yards up the river past the tea garden and then sank in a pool which Mr Northey estimated was some 16ft deep. Seven or eight minutes later 'they saw the huge creature practically beneath where they were standing, making towards the open sea at a fast rate.'

Said Mr Northey: 'The water was disturbed considerably, and w could hear the the wash lapping against the rocks. It was at least 25ft to 30ft long. At first, I thought it was a seal, but a second glance convinced me it was something absolutely different: it was so black and glossy. Its head, several times bigger than a man's, was just above the water. On its back was an extremely huge hump, and flowing behind was a long tail. The strange creature resembled an artist's impression of the Loch Ness monster. It was going just like a submarine on top of the water, and its speed was very fast.'

Seven days later, two visitors staying at the King Arthur's Castle Hotel at Tintagel, saw 'a peculiar animal disporting itself close to the shore in a cove near Tintagel Bay at about 10 o'clock yesterday morning.'

According to them, it resembled in many respects the illustrations they had seen of the Loch Ness monster with a neck which 'appeared to be extraordinarily thin, and, indeed, no thicker than its head.' About two feet of the creature was visible and it appeared that the top of its head and back were a brownish-grey, but the jaw and the underpart of the neck were white.

14

It was a year later that the beast returned to Westcountry waters. It was first spotted by two ladies off Sharkham Point, Devon, and was, according to the witnesses, travelling at about 60mph. It was, they claimed, between 60 and 90 feet long and they declared that they could easily see its fins rising above the water.

A week later, it was near the entrance to Plymouth Sound, according to Mr A.C. Harrison of Noss Mayo. 'While I was walking along Membland Drive early this morning,' he reported on August 24, 1936, 'my attention was drawn seaward by the peculiar cry of the seagulls. At first, I observed what appeared to be a very dark mass below the water surface about a mile from Hillisey Point. I kept it under observation and was surprised to see a huge form come to the surface, showing a length of over 30 feet. To make sure it was not a school of porpoises, I kept watch and noticed that there was no diving, which is peculiar to the porpoise. The thing disappeared but rose again shortly afterwards, and was travelling in an easterly direction.'

Officials at the Plymouth Marine Biological Laboratory, asked again what they thought of the creature, replied that it could have been a basking shark, or 'holiday imagination', while the skipper of a local pleasure steamer, the City of Plymouth, said he thought it was a sunfish because he had seen at least one several times in the vicinity – and they grew to monstrous proportions.

The spate of sightings eased for a while, but the next year it was back – this time at Redlap Cove, near Dartmouth, just before Guy Fawkes Day: it was seen by Mr Harold Groves, head gardener to the well-known actor Cyril Maude. Described as 'a very observant and reliable man', he was pollack fishing in Redlap Cove when his attention was drawn to what looked like a huge conger eel disporting itself on the surface of Start Bay and travelling from west to east. He claimed that it approached the cove as if it intended to pass and the centre of its huge body was high enough out of the water at times for him to see underneath it.

Says the contemporary newspaper report: 'Startled by the

sight, the angler commenced to pick up his tackle, with the intention of going to the cliff-top to get a view of the monster as it passed. By this time the body was actually at the cove-mouth, and the tide was at its highest. As Mr Groves stooped to reach his bait-box, the water broke just a yard or so away from him and a huge head broke surface and reared some two feet out of the water. Mr Groves stared at this remarkable spectacle for quite 30 seconds, when the monster submerged and disappeared.'

Not unnaturally, one supposes, Mr Groves ran all the way home to tell of his close encounter with the monstrous kind. Later, he was to describe his experiences to Mr W.J. Wallis, honorary agent for the British Sea Angler's Society, and said that the head of the monster was not unlike that of a sheep, except that the jaws were longer and more like those of a camel. No fur whatsoever covered the almost-white skin of the face, and except for a tuft of hair on the crown of the head the face was bare. The creature had no ears and its eyes were on the sides of the head and bulged considerably. The tuft of hair on top of the skull was quite thick, but what struck Mr Groves was the distance between the head and the first portion of the body.

Admitting that he would not believe a word of such a story if it had been related to him, Mr Groves said he did not care who doubted his word – the sight would live with him for ever.

There was at least one person who believed him without question – Mr Sidney Field. The day after the incident, he was at Salcombe when he saw a 'strange and formidable creature' swimming lazily towards the mouth of the estuary with its head about a foot above the water. The body was of eel or snake shape and about 20 foot of it showed, while the length of tail which stuck out of the water was 'of a spikey and ribbed nature'. He was so dumbfounded by the sight that he stood transfixed to the spot. By the time he ran to call someone to confirm what he had seen, it had vanished seaward.

A sailor and boatman of many years experience, Mr Field said he was quite accustomed to the sight of basking sharks and seals but 'this was something different in every respect to anything living in the sea' that he had seen before. His only regret was

THE WATER BROKE … and a huge head reared out.

that he had not had someone else to witness the beast.

Between November 1937 and April 1938, the monster went wherever it spent its winter holidays, but it was back in time for Easter, appearing close to Berry Head on April 22 where it was spotted by two Brixham fishermen, Mr Walter Kemp and Mr Glanville Brown, who thought at first that it was a large cask which had been set adrift. 'The strangest thing about it,' said Mr Brown, of Mount Pleasant Road, Brixham, 'was the shape of its head. I never saw anything like it before, and I have been to sea for 40 years – its head was more like that of a hippopotamus.'

Skipper of the Maid Marylon, Mr Kemp was the first to spot the creature as they were returning from fetching their crabbing pots. 'The skipper saw a large fin protruding from the water to a height of three or four feet and we went over to investigate. The head of the thing was well out of the water and this and the fin were the only things visible, but we could see a dim outline of a huge body under the water because we were as close to it as I am to you now. Even when we were close by, and almost looking down upon it, it took no notice whatsoever and just paddled along. The body was about 30 to 40 feet long, much bigger than our launch, which I should imagine it could easily have upset had it come underneath us. The shape was like no ordinary fish, but the head was definitely distinct from the body and had an animal-like appearance.'

Over the years since then, there have been various sighting of the curious beast around the waters of the Westcountry with divers claiming that they have also heard 'a kind of fiendish bark' under the sea which they are convinced does not come from any known sea creature.

A COVE'S SECRET … Does a monster lurk near Cadgwith Cove?

ST MICHAEL'S MOUNT … Did the young Christ visit the Mount as the Cornish tinners' legend claims?

THE
JESUS MYSTERY

THERE is no smoke without fire, according to the old adage, and if that is right then Jesus Christ did step onto the shores of Albion, just as William Blake claims in his famous hymn, *Jerusalem*. And the shores he stepped on to were in the Westcountry.

But it has to be admitted there are no hard facts to say that Jesus ever stepped on the fertile soil of the South West – all we have to rely on are legends, stories, place names, supposition and conjecture. Even some of that evidence comes from unreliable sources – from people who may have wished for their own purposes that Christ was in Britain.

Mystic and Druid leader William Blake certainly believed that Christ had arrived, and was quoting the longheld Westcountry belief that Jesus visited as a small boy, stayed for a while and may even have come back to Britain as a young man to contemplate his future. It may even be that Somerset – and not Israel – is the seat of Christianity, and that a great deal of Christian doctrine owes its foundations to the Druids of the South West.

The legend says that Christ came to Britain with his uncle, Joseph of Arimathea, a wealthy tin trader who came to the Westcountry to take ingots of the precious metal back to the Phoenicians.

Allegedly, Jesus came ashore in several places in Cornwall and Somerset – but never in Devon, because there was no lead or tin mining nearly 2,000 years ago in the area – including Penzance, Marazion, St Michael's Mount, Mousehole, Ding Dong Mine,

Rock in the Camel Estuary, Redruth, Carnon Downs, Nancledra, St Day and Falmouth, St Just-in-Roseland, Polruan-by-Fowey, Looe Island and Looe itself in Cornwall and in Priddy, Burnham-on-Sea, Pilton and, of course, Glastonbury in Somerset. There are also claims that he visited Hurst Castle in Hampshire and the Isle of Wight, thought to be the Ictis of Roman tradition, and there are one or two legends of Christ landing in Ireland.

But to unravel the mystery, we have to go back to the very beginnings, for there are several important principles which have to be established.

First, it has to be established, if possible, whether Joseph was in fact the uncle. Secondly, it has to be verified that Joseph traded tin with Britain. Thirdly, it has to be possible for Christ to

ST MICHAEL'S MOUNT TODAY ... One of Cornwall's famous landmarks.

have been 'missing' from Israel for the period in question.

The period in question was the Dark Ages as far as history is concerned – in fact, for the first five centuries of Britain's Christian life, the history books are almost totally blank. The first British historian was Gildas, who lived between AD 516-570, although some scholars claim to have found a few scraps of information in the works of Taliesin and some of the Welsh bards.

For any early information about the history of England, scholars are obliged to scour the writings of Julius Caesar, Tacitus, Dion Cassius and other Roman writers. But all these recorders saw Britain as enemy territory, with Caesar claiming that the Britons were barbarians. In fact, the Britons had a well-organised social structure and possessed a high degree of culture, as well as religious beliefs under the Druids which were far more superior to the Romans in many respects.

Early British history comes from oral tradition, for it was not properly recorded until some 1,000 years after the birth of Christ.

This oral tradition, of course, was no doubt embellished in the retelling but there is every reason to believe that the stories sprang from a germ of truth.

The Rev H.A. Lewis, MA, examined the evidence earlier this century and published several pamphlets – *The Christ Child at Lammana* (Looe), *Ab Antiquo* and *Christ in Cornwall?* – while the pamphlet *Did Our Lord Visit Britain, as they say in Cornwall and Somerset?* by the Rev C.C. Dobson, MA, ran into seven editions and seven reprints.

He says: 'I claim that the legendary visit of Our Lord to Britain, and to Cornwall in particular, comes through all tests remarkably unscathed, leaving all reasonable people with the conviction that it may have been, and many of us, who have given years of study to the subject, the growing faith that it is probably true.'

The legend of the visit, say both authors, persists most strongly in the mining districts of Cornwall and the adjacent ports from which tin was exported before and during the first century

THE CAMEL ESTUARY … Joseph and Jesus reputedly stopped for water at the Jesus Well in Rock.

AD. It is conspicuous by its absence in other areas – particularly that of Devon – and the legend is not usually found in monastic areas, except Glastonbury where the legend surrounds the visit of his uncle more than anything else. Says the Rev Lewis: 'Even at Glastonbury, the legend perpetuated and embellished by the monks of the Middle Ages was about Joseph of Arimathea, rather than about Our Lord, as the holy visitor.'

Surprisingly, he adds, the story of Christ's visit to St Michael's Mount is expressly mentioned in the tinner's version of the legend, but was not continued through the monastic connections with the Mount. If it had been a monastic legend, would not the monks have perpetuated the story of a visit by Christ?

Another indication that it was an oral tradition of the people, says the Rev Lewis, a former Vicar of St Martins on the Isles of Scilly, is the way the legend 'is given in the simplest language, without any of the "artistic detail" so dear to the monastic legend-mongers, but so damaging to the value and credibility of many of the stories in, say, the "Acta Santorum". The legend of the Holy Visit itself is not found in the elaborate romances of the Arthurian cycle, though there is indirect support for it in the claim of the greatest knights of the Round Table to descent from Joseph of Arimathea, who is closely associated with the legend, and who provides an important clue to its credibility.'

The Rev Lewis claims that 'there is not one word in the Gospel narrative which in any way disproves' the legends and that the omission of direct or indirect reference 'is of little value, in view of the fact that there is, I imagine, only one alternative legend with regard to the eighteen years of Our Lord's boyhood and early manhood, viz, that he spent all his time at Nazareth as a carpenter, and there is certainly *no more* support for this belief in the story of the Evangelists. On the contrary, I consider that the account of his visit to Nazareth during the ministry fits in far better with the possibility of a prolonged absence, for he appears in the Synagogue as, at least, a comparative stranger. Even if he had made Nazareth his home for all those eighteen years, there would still have been plenty of *time* for a visit to Britain, if the *opportunity* was there.'

Joseph, he contends, provided that opportunity.

He goes on: 'Archaeology is showing us more and more the absurdity of the old idea that the Britons in the time of Christ were wild, painted savages. The finds in the lake villages of Meare and Glastonbury show a remarkable degree of culture and art, and so do the excavations ... in the old 'castles' of Cornwall. It is more than possible that the Phoenician and Hebrew traders had many friends in these islands of a culture little (if any) inferior to their own.'

And to add to the tale, the Rev Dobson claims that not only did Jesus visit the South West as a small boy but he returned later in life to Glastonbury immediately prior to starting his Ministry in the Holy Land at the age of 30. He asks in his pamphlet: 'Was there a motive in his visiting Britain, and actually ministering here, without revealing his identity as the future saviour of the world? In doing so, did he effect the divine programme for the Christian age about to begin?'

And following the death of Christ on Calvary, Joseph of Arimathea came back to Glastonbury to settle, establishing the first true Christian church on what is now the site of the Abbey ruins, it is claimed, bringing with him the Holy Grail used by Christ to serve the wine at the Last Supper. At the same time, he also struck his staff into the ground on Wearyall Hall where the everlasting thorn tree grows.

To give any credence to the stories, however, we must go back and start establishing facts, and the first one is: was there a trade in tin and lead between Cornwall and Somerset and Phoenicia?

As early as 455 BC, Herodotus mentions the British Isles as the Tin Islands, or Cassiterides, while Pytheas (352-323 BC) speaks of the tin trade. Polybius (circa 160 BC) also mentioned the business connections, while Diodorus Siculus gives a detailed description, including the fact that the people of the island were particularly friendly and had good manners and that the tin mined in the island was beaten into squares and carried to an island called Ictis, which was joined to the mainland at low tide. Many scholars claim that Ictis is St Michael's Mount, although others have suggested it might be Falmouth – or even

GLASTONBURY ABBEY … An engraving from an earlier age.

the Isle of Wight. From there it was shipped across the English Channel to Morlaix, or some other port in Brittany, and transported across France and through Gaul to the Rhone Estuary by packhorse to the ports of Marseilles and Narbonne, thus avoiding a hazardous trip across the Bay of Biscay for small craft. From there, it was shipped to Phoenicia.

There are, of course, hundreds of ancient tin workings in Cornwall – most of them 'lost' in the sense that there are no maps of them – and British and Cornish historians are of the opinion that tin mines existed in the South West peninsula as early as 1500 BC. States Sir Edward Creasy in his *History of England*: 'The British mines mainly supplied the glorious adornment of Solomon's Temple.'

At the same time as the tin streaming and adit mining for tin was going on in Cornwall, lead, copper and other metals which form alloys with tin were being extracted in the Mendips. Proof of this was the ancient pig of lead which was discovered bearing the stamp of Britannicus, the son of Claudius, showing that lead was being brought to the surface and smelted at the time of Christ.

The lead mines at Priddy were certainly in existence before the Romans began to exploit them in about 50 AD.

Says the Rev L.S. Lewis, a former Vicar of Glastonbury, in *St Joseph of Arimathea at Glastonbury*: 'If I were to venture to reconstruct a trading voyage of the tin merchants from materials available, I should say that it probably began at Tyre or Joppa, that the merchants disembarked at Narbonne, and that they travelled overland from thence to Morlaix, re-embarked for the crossing of the Channel to the Fal, and, after calling at various trading places along the Cornish coast, proceeded, either by sea or land, to their terminus in the Mendips.'

If they went by land, of course, they would have had to cross Devon – surely a legend of Joseph or Christ would have built up if either of them had travelled across the region? The fact that there is no Devon legend would seem to suggest that they went by sea, around Land's End, travelling up the North Cornish coast to the Somerset mines.

Having established the probability of commerce between Britain and Phoenicia the next step is to try and establish whether Joseph of Arimathea was a tin trader.

There is no definite reference to him as such in the Bible, but he is described as wealthy. Westcountry tradition says that Joseph's trade was in transporting the metal, and according to the Rev Dobson 'tin miners were wont to sing a quaint song, the refrain of which ran: Joseph was in the tin trade,' although he gives no further lines of the song. The Rev Lewis also reports hearing the song from miners recalling their days at the turn of the century, but can only add a second line which said: 'And the miners loved him well', and recollected that one woman told him that she was sure it was 'about his coming in a ship'.

In 1916 Dr Henry Jenner, then the Grand Bard of the Cornish Gorsedd, was convinced that the oral tradition had a basis in fact and twice wrote articles for the *Western Morning News* on the subject, as well as a full article about the exploits of St Joseph of Arimathea, for *Pax*, the journal of the Benedictines, in which he pointed out the difficulty of finding 'an adequate reason' why Joseph should be singled out for this treatment 'unless it happened to be the literal and accurate truth'. The invocation, 'Joseph was in the tin trade,' by the miners, he says, affords some grounds for belief that he actually was. He goes on to quote Mr Bailie Hamilton as having heard from the foreman of a mine in Cornwall the explanation for the song: 'One of these (traditions) is that St Joseph of Arimathea, the rich man of the Gospels, made his money in the tin trade between Phoenicia and Cornwall. We also have a story that he made several voyages to Britain in his own ships, and that on one occasion he brought with him the child Christ and his mother as passengers, and landed them at St Michael's Mount in Cornwall.'

The Isles of Scilly vicar said he had heard similar stories from local people in various parts of Cornwall in the earlier part of this century, particularly between the ancient tin streaming districts of Carnon Downs and the creeks of the River Fal, from where the tin would have been shipped abroad to the inhabitants of the so-called civilised world, where the tin would have been

THE JESUS WELL … The traditional site is carefully preserved.

amalgamated with copper – possibly mined at Caradon or in the Mendips – to form bronze, a study metal for weapons of war.

He claims that the stories of Joseph's visit to the Westcountry are so strongly attested to and widespread 'that it may be practically regarded as an established fact. If he had been engaged in the tin trade, we have an explanation of his selection of Cornwall for his place of retreat when forced to flee Palestine,' he explains. But that claim will be hotly contested by Somerset later on, as we shall see ...

In the meantime, we must establish some sort of relationship between Jesus and Joseph – the reason why Joseph would volunteer to take Our Lord on such an arduous trip away from his mother, the Virgin Mary.

It is an old Eastern tradition that Christ was the nephew of Joseph, but there is no direct statement to that effect in the Bible. It may be inferred, however, from two distinct events in the life of Jesus. The first is Our Lord's first Passover at the age of 12, although Joseph (Christ's earthly father) and Mary set off for home without the young lad, and it was three days later that he was found. Where had he been in the intervening days – who had fed him – who had given him shelter? The explanation is that he was staying with a relative, and as John the Baptist was his cousin and only a few months older than Jesus and was also attending his first Passover, the likelihood is that that relative was him.

The road between Jerusalem and Nazareth passes through Arimathea – the wealthy counsellor's home – or Ramallah as it is called today, and it would be a natural stopping place for anyone travelling between the two towns. Says the Rev Dobson: 'They would spend the last night of the journey there at their uncle's house. Joseph would either have already preceded them to the city for the feast, or be expecting them there, and conduct them for the remaining eight miles of their journey.' The Rev. Dobson says the feast lasted seven days, but Joseph and Mary set off for home after five days leaving Jesus behind – with whom? When he did not appear, they retraced their footsteps and found the 12-year-old at the Synagogue attending one of the lectures given by the Rabbis. 'How is it that ye sought me?' he asks, surprised. 'Wist ye not that I must be about my father's business?'

The second, and more plausible, clue comes after Christ is nailed to the cross at the age of 33. Joseph of Arimathea goes to Pontius Pilate and asks for his body, which he then buried in his own private sepulchre in his garden. Would he have done that for a stranger, particularly one who had been condemned to death by the mob?

Says the Rev Dobson: 'For anyone to reverence the remains of one thus nationally condemned, and regarded moreover as a criminal, guilty of the most serious crime known to the Jews – that of claiming to be the Messiah and Divine – was to incur the most serious risk of public hostility under ordinary circumstances.'

There were, he says, two places reserved outside of Jerusalem for the burying of criminals and in normal circumstances the elders would have demanded that he be buried there. But both Roman and Jewish law laid it down as a duty for the nearest relative to dispose of the dead, irrespective of how they died. If Joseph was given permission to take the body, was it because he was a relative and only obeying the law?

The last hurdle is: was there time for Jesus to visit Cornwall and Somerset? There is certainly a massive gap between the ages of 12 and 30 but to claim that he was in the Westcountry can only be supported by legends and stories, although John the Baptist did express surprise when he arrived to be baptised. 'Art thou he that should come, or look we for another?' If Jesus had been in Palestine and they were cousins, would they not have met at the feasts which they were bound to attend under Mosaic law? And where was Joseph of Arimathea during this time?

If he were the uncle of Jesus whose earthly father was dead, it would be natural for him to assume the role of adoptive father under Mosaic law. Most scholars agree that the Virgin Mary became a widow while Jesus was a youth and the family moved from Nazareth to Capernaum – and it would be natural for Joseph to take his 'son' with him on any venture.

All the stories agree that Jesus and Joseph called in to the Mount's Bay area of Cornwall, may well have sailed up the

South Coast as far as Looe calling in at Falmouth – the main port of the county even at that time – and then voyaged around the county to the Camel Estuary where they stopped for water at a place now named Jesus Well at Rock and then progressed on to the Summer-land (Somerset as we call it today). His first visit would attract little attention. But it probably made an impression on the young man – this land of lakes with islands looming out of the mist as it rolled in from the sea.

According to the stories, Jesus returned to Glastonbury and on the site of what is now the ruined abbey, built a small house of mud and wattle. Here he stayed in quiet meditation for several years, attracting little attention as he went about a hermit-like existence. No one would have noticed his departure, either. It was only when Joseph came back to Somerset and told of his final three years in Palestine that they would remember him. Joseph, it is claimed, turned Jesus's old house into a church and supposedly encased it in lead to preserve it against the elements. At the same time, he drove his staff into Wearyall Hill where it took root and became the Holy Thorn: certainly the thorn tree is similar to species which grow in Palestine. Hamish Miller and Paul Broadhurst, however, claim in *The Sun and The Serpent*: 'The original tree was evidently tall and double-trunked, blossoming on Christmas Day. Its mystique was unrivalled, famous across the land, with James I and other monarchs treasuring cuttings from it. It was evidently attacked by Puritans, and ultimately destroyed during the Civil War. The original thorn, *Crataegus oxyacanth praecox*, now has many offspring in the area, including specimens at St John's Church and in the Abbey grounds, and every year as part of archaic ritual a sprig is sent to the reigning sovereign. This seems yet another of those peculiar Glastonbury coincidences that lead you to believe that there might be more to such legends than meets the eye, for this particular species grows in the region of the Holy Land and may well have been planted by a pilgrim or a crusader, if not by Joseph himself.'

Joseph is also supposed to have brought with him the chalice used at the Last Supper and to have buried it below the Tor,

RECONSTRUCTION ... A painting by V J Lee of a reconstructed mud and wattle hut of Early Christian times.

along with two silver cruets, one containing some of the blood which trickled down Jesus's side as he lay dying on the cross, which is why the water runs red, and the other containing some of his sweat, which is why the other spring in the vicinity runs crystal clear or slightly blue.

And there are the hints of the church which was built by Christ at Glastonbury, referred to by St Augustine in a letter to Pope Gregory in which he states: 'In the Western confines of Britain there is a certain royal island of large extent, surrounded by water, abounding in all the beauties of nature and necessaries of life. In the first Neophites of Catholic law, God beforehand acquainting them, found a Church constructed by no human art, but divinely constructed for the salvation of his people. The Almighty made it manifest by many miracles and mysterious visitations that He continues to watch over it as sacred to Himself, and to Mary, the Mother of God.'

St Augustine, of course, arrived in Britain in AD 597 and expected to find the whole island pagan. In the Westcountry, however, he found a powerful British church with its own bishops already in existence. It was only in the east of the land, where the Saxons had invaded and settled, that the pagans existed.

His assertion that the church was dedicated to the Virgin Mary is confirmed by the writings of Maelgwyn of Llandaff in AD 450 and by William of Malmesbury who saw the *Ealde Chirche* before it. The subsequent Abbey built around it was destroyed by fire on May 25, 1184. Malmesbury had access to the copious records and books built up over 1,000 years by the Abbey monks and we are lucky that he was able to quote from many of them before they, too, were destroyed in the blaze. In fact, he gives fifteen pages of information 'gathered from a mass of evidences and documents of no small credit' which establish, among many other things, that the wattle church existed.

Even the Domesday Book of 1086 gives more than a hint of the holiness of the area, for it records that: 'The Domus Dei, in the great Monastery of Glastinbury, called the Secret of Our Lord. This Glastinbury church possesses in its own Villa XII hides of land which have never been taxed,' which correspond to the 12 hides of land said to have been given by King Arviragus to Joseph and his eleven companions who settled there after the death of Christ. The fact that the land remained inviolate for more than 1,000 years is, says the Rev Dobson, 'strong witness to the coming of Joseph to Glastonbury, but also that special sanctity and reverence was attached to the gift.' Domus Dei is also interpreted as 'Home of God.'

Maelgwyn of Llandaff records that Joseph and his companions were buried at Glastonbury – 'He lies in the southern angle of the bifurcated line of the Oratorium of the Adorable Virgin' – with the epitaph of his grave reading: 'Ad Britannos veni post Christum spelivi. Docui. Quievi,' translated as: 'I came to the Britons after I buried Christ. I taught. I rest.'

According to Glastonbury records, Joseph's body remained buried until AD 1345 when Edward III gave his assent to John Bloom of London to dig for it, with the consent of the Abbots and Monks. The body, according to Lincolnshire monks in 1367, was found and placed in a silver casket let into a stone sarcophagus, which was placed in the east end of Joseph's Chapel where it became a place of pilgrimage. It was moved, according to records, in 1662 when the chapel became partly ruined and owing to Puritan fanaticism present at the time, secretly removed to the Parish Church churchyard by night. It was reburied with the initials JA – supposedly to stand for John Allen – and finally located in 1928 by the then vicar who had it moved into the church. Its construction, it is said, confirms the accounts of a silver casket which could be raised and lowered and it is supposed to show other marks of identity.

Place names also provide some very good clues to history – for instance, Penzance is interpreted as Holy Headland and may well have got its name from its association with Jesus, although there are many people who claim that it is associated with John the Baptist: one or two wood carvings of John the Baptist's head displayed on a plate hang above house doorways in the town, and the town also has its Market Jew Street. Marazion (Mount Zion) has Hebrew connections; Essa at Saltash and Polruan, might suggest the name of Jesus in Hebrew (Yesup), while the Jesus Well at Rock has a unique dedication. Dozens of other places in Somerset have connections in their names – Paradise, for instance, is found in several places.

One intriguing little story concerns Lammana (Looe), which was a priory of Glastonbury before the Norman Conquest. It comes in a book written by J. Robert Hunt – *A Story of Looe Island*. Mr Hunt's 1966 book rather romantically tells the story of Jesus and Joseph landing on the island – complete with quotes from Jesus and Joseph!

In the story, Joseph leaves Jesus on St George's Island – because Looe is a bit of a rough place – telling him to watch for his fire signal on top of Caradon Hill, where he will be collecting copper from the miners. Left on his own, Jesus falls in love with

The HISTORY of that Holy Disciple
JOSEPH *of* *Arimathea,*

Wherein is contained,

The true Account of his Birth, his Parents, his Country, his Education, his Piety; and how he begged of PONTIUS PILATE the Body of Our Blessed Saviour, after his Crucifixion, which he buried in a new Sepulchre of his own.

Also the Occasion of his Coming to ENGLAND,

Where he first preached the Gospel at Glastenbury in Somersetshire; and where is still growing that noted White-Thorn, which buds every Christmas-Day in the Morning, blossoms at Noon, and fades at Night, on the Place where he pitched his Staff in the Ground.

With a full Relation of his Death and Burial.

FROM THE ABBEY … The first page of a six-page 17th century pamphlet in the collection owned by Glastonbury Abbey.

37

the little island and on his return to Palestine tells his mother of his adventures. He is then asked by Joseph of Arimathea to undertake another little trip for him – to Tibet. There he recounts his stay on Looe Island to the monks, who duly record it on one of their scrolls. This is rediscovered some years later, leading to four monks making the journey to Cornwall where they set up a Christian monastery on the island.

This may be a little too fanciful for serious investigators into the Jesus mystery, but it does show how legends begin – for the story has been repeated orally already as if it were the truth when, in fact, there is no evidence whatsoever to say that it happened.

Whatever the actual truth is of Jesus's visit to Cornwall and Somerset, it is a beautiful legend which will never die.

THE WHITE RABBIT

WHEREVER you look in the Westcountry, there are stories, legends and reports of ghosts – and mostly they revolve around people. But there are also thousands of stories about ghost animals, and one of them is the ghostly white rabbit which stalks the long grass of Egloshayle Churchyard near Wadebridge.

No one is quite certain when or where the story originated, but it was certainly old when author Arthur Norway – related to the ill-fated Nevell Norway and world famous author Nevil Shute – began compiling his notes for his book *Highways and Byways in Devon and Cornwall*, first published in 1897.

The rabbit, he asserts, only appears on nights with a full moon and can be seen gambolling about in an open space beside the churchyard wall. 'A pretty, long-eared rabbit with pink eyes, like any child's pet escaped from its hutch,' proclaims the author. 'It goes loppeting around among the grasses by the corner of the marsh, and if anyone should pass, will sit and look at him with fearless eyes. And well it may. It has nothing to dread from any-one dwelling in those parts. No villager would attempt to catch it. No boy would aim a blow at it.'

And with very good reason. It could be the last thing they did. For the rabbit had a nasty habit of making things backfire on anyone who would make it a tasty addition to the Sunday lunch. It's better to stay vegetarian if you want to live in Egloshayle!

'If anyone walking late sees the white rabbit lopping about at his heels, he makes no effort to drive it away, but quickens his

BY THE WATER ... The church by the River Camel – the scene of an extraordinary haunting.

pace, and hopes that some good angel may stand between him and harm,' says Mr Norway.

But there had to be one person who took the risk, and he was a postman, late on his rounds. He became terrified when the rabbit began to follow him and struck out with an oak cudgel. 'He felt the stick fall on the soft back of the rabbit', claims Mr Norway, 'such a blow as might have killed a much larger animal. But the rabbit lopped on as if nothing had happened. The cudgel it was which was broken – shivered into splinters, as if it had struck upon a rock.'

The postman got off with just a fright, but not everyone did, for Norway claims that in his grandfather's day a deliberate attempt was made to meddle with the creature. It was perpetrated by a stranger to the legend.

The story goes that a group of young men were drinking at the Molesworth Arms Hotel in the centre of the town. As the evening wore on, the talk grew more and more outrageous, until someone at last spoke of the white rabbit.

The stranger instantly began to jeer. Fancy country yokels believing such a story – it would be laughed at where he lived, but in a pokey country town people had nothing better to do than to listen and put credence in old women's tales. He would like to go out and shoot it for them!

One of the company drew aside the pub shutter and looked out. The street was as bright as day and overhead the full moon was sailing in a cloudless sky. 'Tha'd best go now,' he told the stranger. 'When the moon shines like this, tha'll find the rabbit by the church.'

Reports have it that a gun was hanging on the wall and it was taken down and loaded amid a babble of jeers and angry murmurings. But the crowd escorted the stranger into Molesworth Street and watched him stride down the moonlit street towards the ancient bridge across the River Camel, whistling cheerfully to himself. As soon as he was out of sight, the crowd hurried to their beers.

One would imagine laughter must have split the air at the Molesworth as jovial locals downed their ales waiting for the stranger's return, but instead there was an air of uneasiness in the room. No one seemed to inclined to sit down; they moved restlessly about the bar, until one of them went out and looked into the street.

'The others asked eagerly if he heard anything,' reports Norway, recalling the story his grandfather had told him, though they knew the stranger could not have reached the church; and then one suggested it was a shame to allow a man who had no knowledge of danger to encounter it alone. The others agreed as readily as men will when they have done what does not please them, and without more delay they set off in a body.'

They trudged along in silence across the bridge and into Egloshayle Road towards the outskirts of the town beside what was then a marsh. But as they neared the church they heard the sound of a gunshot, and instantly a loud scream.

With fast-beating hearts, they ran on, but when they reached the low walls surrounding the church there was no one and nothing to be seen. They ran around calling out to the stranger, but got no reply. 'He was not in the lane, nor on the high road, nor on the marsh where, under the bright moonlight, the motion of a waterhen could have been seen with ease,' proclaims Norway. 'At last, one of the searchers leapt upon the churchyard wall, and sprang down on the inner side, calling on his friends to follow him. There they found him, lying dead, with one barrel of his gun discharged and the contents in his body.'

Ever since then, asserts the author, on moonlit nights the stranger can still be seen leaning over the wall aiming an ancient flintlock gun at some object which moves quickly in the long grass.

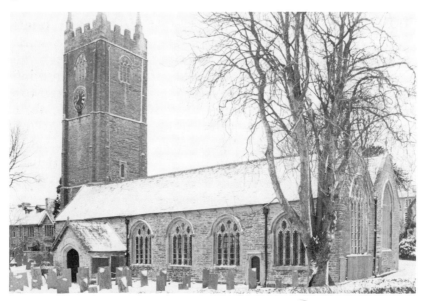

THE CHURCHYARD SECRET … 'they found him lying dead…'

DISAPPEARING DORIS

THERE was something decidedly odd about the disappearance of 43-year-old Mrs Doris Symonds, who it was claimed walked out on her husband during an intended visit to Cornwall from their Newton Abbot home. According to her husband, Captain Godfrey Bidewell Symonds, a military adviser in the Persian Gulf, the attractive former Wren simply walked off into the distance when they stopped at Plymouth and was never seen again.

It lead to one of the most prolonged 'missing persons' hunts ever mounted in the Westcountry – and ended in what became known as the 'murder without a body' trial.

It began when Mrs Symonds – affectionately known as Phill because her maiden name was Phillips and she hated the name Doris – and her husband, set off in June 1963 for a weekend in Cornwall. She never arrived. Instead, she walked out on her husband and four-year-old son, Martin, telephoning later to simply say: 'I'm off.' At least, that was how Captain Symonds explained her disappearance to police when they questioned him.

The Westcountry was scoured for Mrs Symonds; appeals were made in newspapers and on radio, relatives and friends were contacted for the least scrap of information, but it was as if she had simply walked off the face of the earth. After a while, the hunt died down and Captain Symonds divorced his wife on the grounds of desertion and remarried.

Her brother, Mr Leonard Phillips, of Stoke Poges,

Buckinghamshire, however, did not know that she had disappeared and after not hearing from her for five years, began a two-year hunt to find out what had happened.

It led to renewed interest in the case when Detective Chief Superintendent Proven Sharpe – one of the most tenacious detectives ever to operate in the South West – revealed that he had a massive dossier on the case, that a detective inspector had just returned from Dusseldorf where he had interviewed Army personnel who had known the couple when they were stationed in Germany, and that Interpol was helping him to try to solve the mystery. Proven Sharpe did not say so at the time, but he was convinced that the Army captain had murdered his wife: all he needed were the right clues.

In November 1971, he told the press: 'We have been making inquiries which are likely to go on for some time. We are keeping an open mind as we realise her disappearance could well have been a domestic matter, and if that is so we should like her to get in touch with us because we don't want to waste our time. We should also like to hear from anyone who has been in touch with the former Mrs Symonds during the past seven years.'

It was then revealed detectives had interviewed a number of people at Rawlinson Barracks, Denbury, near Newton Abbot, where the couple had lived in a service house at Aller while their son went to school at Wolborough.

Captain Symonds moved out of the house he and Phill had occupied because, he told friends, it held too many memories for him, and moved to Bideford, North Devon, leaving a few weeks later to take up a post in the Persian Gulf while his second wife remained at home. He returned to Britain in September the following year – only to be met at Stansted Airport by airport police who detained him to await the arrival of Proven Sharpe with a warrant for his arrest. Proven Sharpe had been at Heathrow Airport waiting for him to return, but the aircraft had been diverted because of fog.

The next day, he appeared before Newton Abbot Magistrates' Court facing a charge of murder.

44

THE HUSBAND ...
Captain Geoffrey Symonds

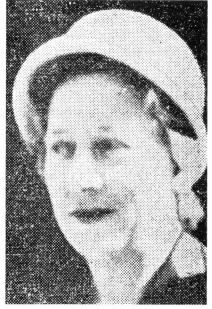

THE MISSING WIFE ...
Mrs Doris Symonds

45

Friends and colleagues rallied round when he applied for bail, the magistrates being told that Captain Symonds had already returned home at Christmas to try and help the police trace his former wife. He was, said solicitor Mr Michael Brabin, appealing for his release, an MBE and was willing to stand surety for the total value of his house, while many friends, including his former commanding officer, would stand surety for him.

'A lot of people are putting a lot of faith in him and are prepared to back him,' Mr Brabin said, adding that police had carried out extensive enquiries since Mrs Symonds vanished and had interviewed more than 300 people. Now facing a murder charge, Captain Symonds wanted the public to help him find his ex-wife, who he hoped would come forward when she realised the serious consequences facing her former husband.

Proven Sharpe, however, opposed bail on the grounds that the captain was facing a serious charge and that he had contacts in the Middle East, which was outside the jurisdiction of British justice, and the police feared the possibility that he would not return. When he had come back to Britain at Christmas, the police had not completed their investigations and had no power to stop him from going back. The bench remanded him in custody, but granted him legal aid to cover two counsel. The dapper military man – who appeared in court wearing a smart black blazer and his regimental tie – must have wondered on that September day in 1972 how an incident nine years ago had suddenly sprung to life.

He was back in court a week later, with crowds four deep lining the pavement outside the courthouse to get a glimpse of him as he arrived under heavy police escort and hand-cuffed to a uniformed officer, and again his solicitor pleaded for him to be released on bail. Captain Symonds turned in court and blew a kiss to his second wife, Freda, as she sat crying in the public seats, little realising at that stage that Proven Sharpe thought she was at the bottom of the mystery.

Mr Brabin told the court during the defendant's 30-minute

appearance that it was unusual to apply for bail on a murder charge, but added: 'It is the very seriousness of the charge that makes it imperative for Captain Symonds to be at liberty to help in his own defence.' He claimed that the case had already set at least one legal record – he believed it was the longest time span between an investigation beginning and a charge being laid.

He again said Captain Symonds would answer his bail, and added that he would also surrender his passport, report to the police daily and put the full value of his home up as surety. Mr Brabin claimed that no substantial evidence had been brought against his client: no body had been found and there was nothing to suggest that the first Mrs Symonds was not still alive. His claim was that she had left him nine years ago while in Plymouth.

County prosecutor Mr Neville Jennings claimed it was naive of anyone to believe that surrendering a passport prevented a person from going abroad, and Captain Symonds had many contacts in the Middle East, particularly in Abu Dhabi, where there were no extradition proceedings. His contention was that the prosecution had substantial evidence that he had murdered Doris Irene Symonds sometime between June 7 and 11, 1963.

The prosecution claimed they would be ready to proceed with the case by Christmas, but Captain Symonds remained in custody until February the next year before he appeared before judge and jury. In the meantime, Mr Philip Browning, for the Director of Public Prosecution, Sir Michael Havers, who had personally given the go-ahead for the trial after studying the police evidence, was still objecting to bail applications, with Mr Brabin claiming it was 'a most complex case' with the defence likely to call some 45 witnesses and the prosecution any number between 90 and 200 – they had interviewed more than 400 people.

In the meantime, Mr Brabin appealed to the public for help, particularly over a snapshot of a woman taken in St Helier, Jersey, in 1964. The woman was described as being middle aged, reserved and on her own, and had her picture taken by a holiday photographer claiming her name was Mrs Doris Symonds and that her husband was a military man. Two weeks later, his appeal was answered – it was not Mrs Symonds.

But then another hopeful clue was discovered: a letter to *The Times* from a Johann Hellmutt who claimed that he saw a person answering the description of Captain Symonds' wife in 1965 – two years after he was alleged to have killed her and spirited away her body. The meeting, said the letter writer, had taken place in Bodiam, Sussex. Unfortunately for Captain Symonds, Mr Helmutt did not give his address and although police descended on the Hastings, Rye and Battle areas to make inquiries, no trace of him was found – even when the police issued a copy of his signature to every newspaper.

The letter, posted in Bedford, said the writer had met a woman claiming to be Mrs Symonds in a car park at Bodiam Castle in the late summer of 1964 when she was having difficulty with her Hillman car. She had told him her name and he gave her a lift to Hastings. On the way, she said she was going to live in Jersey and that her husband was serving somewhere in the Middle East.

With the trial set to begin on February 13, 1973, Captain Symonds must have been thinking of his future as he languished in Exeter Prison. At the Crown Court, officials were thinking of the future as well: they were contemplating what they thought might turn out to be the longest and costliest trial ever to take place in the Westcountry – it had already been decided to call 70 potential jurors to select the final 12 good men and true, 20 or so local and national newspapers had requested seats where there was normally only room for five, and then there was the interest from the public who would have to be controlled or swamp the public gallery.

When 49-year-old Captain Symonds was led up from the holding cells into the dock to plead 'not guilty' to the murder of his former wife, he was facing an all-male jury and standing before Mr Justice Bristow at the Castle, Exeter, with Mr L

EXETER PRISON ... Where Captain Symonds spent long weeks before and during his trial.

Hampden Inskip QC and Mr Martin Tucker for the prosecution, and Mr James Comym QC, Mr David Owen Thomas QC and Mr Graham Neville – later to become Judge Graham Neville – for the defence.

In his opening address, Mr Inskip told the jury that they would have to be sure that Mrs Symonds was dead, and had to be sure that Symonds had caused her death. He claimed that the totality of the circumstances could leave no one in any doubt that Mrs Symonds had been dead since the weekend of June 8-9, 1963, and that it was Symonds who had caused her death.

He said Mrs Symonds had been born in December, 1921, the youngest of four children. During the war she joined the WRNS and became an officer. It was on her way home from Columbo in 1946 that she had met a young warrant officer, aged 23, and fell in love. She and Captain Symonds married less than a year later.

Describing Doris Symonds as a stable, quiet person with a kindly disposition, introvert and with an intense desire to help her husband on his way in his service career, he said she had described herself to a friend as 'a bit of a cold fish, not largely enthusiastic about the physical side of marriage, undemonstrative in love but with a deep affection for her husband.' On the other hand, Captain Symonds was totally different – a warrant officer who was efficient, enthusiastic and an extrovert. It was, he said, an oddly contrasting marriage which, to outward observers, bore the test and stresses of time well for many years.

But that, he said, was a lie, for when their son was born on November 9, 1960, Captain Symonds had already started his affair with Miss Freda Bennallack, the manageress of the NAAFI in Herford. The jury would hear, he said, of Symonds being seen coming from her quarters at night. And another witness would tell how Captain Symonds and his wife went home on leave in January, 1961, with Miss Bennallack terminating her contract on the same day and returning home to Cornwall.

After a day or so at an address in London, his wife went to her brother's home and Symonds left to return to Germany. In fact, for the rest of his leave it was obvious that he had joined Freda Bennallack in Cornwall, said Mr Inskip. It was obvious, he said, that Symonds wanted to be with her rather than his wife and in fact had admitted to police during one of his interviews that he had asked his wife for a divorce. Posted to Dembury Camp at Newton Abbot in March, 1962, it soon became obvious to other officers and subordinates that there were frequent letters going to Miss Bennallack in Cornwall, and equally frequent letters returning from Liskeard. The letters were numbered at the top and it was the belief of many people that he was 'carrying on a liaison' with a woman in Cornwall. The rumour increased when Captain Symonds declared that none of his personal correspondence was to be sent to his home.

Some time later, said Mr Inskip, Captain Symonds told a

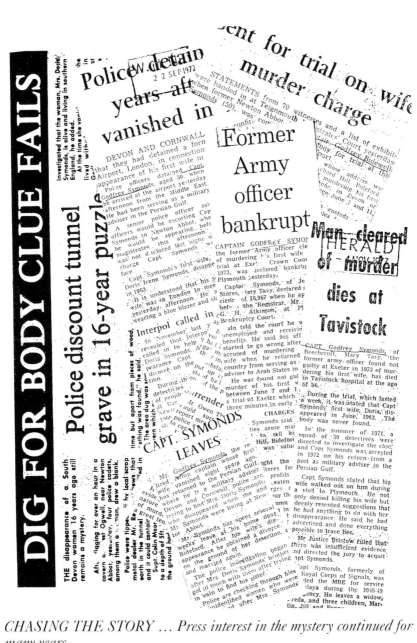

CHASING THE STORY … Press interest in the mystery continued for many years.

quartermaster-sergeant at the camp that 'it had all blown up' and that his wife had found out about his girlfriend. This, he contended, was Symonds' way of paving the way to say: 'She has left me' after the fateful weekend.

Paving the way for the weekend, he had told his house-keeper that he was taking his wife to Cornwall at her request and asked her to look after little Martin. Said Mr Inskip: 'It seems a little improbably that Phill would ask to be taken down to Cornwall where she knew Freda was living.' But on the following Monday, he returned alone, telling the house-keeper that his wife had been called away to London where her sister was desperately ill. This, he said, was untrue, and Symonds had admitted as much to the police. Equally, he had told another person that his wife had left him, that he did not know what he was going to do, and that his world had tumbled about him. It was all just so much humbug, said Mr Inskip.

From that time on, Captain Symonds gave many different versions of what happened to his wife, but they all involved her getting out of the car, doing some shopping and making a telephone call. He, in the meantime, simply sat in the car and remembered her coming back and saying something which he really did not listen to, and then her 'disappearing into the blue'. He claimed to have sat in the car for some time after that and to have made one telephone call to the local hospital to see if his wife had been taken there, but did not contact the police.

He claimed, however, to have heard from his wife on June 11 when she telephoned and said: 'I'm off.' It was a telephone call that was never made, said Mr Inskip, and was an invention to try and give some support to his claim that she was still alive.

Mr Inskip led the attack by telling the jury that the prosecution contended that nearly 10 years ago, Symonds murdered his first wife after they left their home near Newton Abbot to spend the weekend in Cornwall. He admitted that no body had ever been found, but since that weekend no relative or friend had heard a word from Doris Symonds, either by telephone, letter or substantial rumour.

He claimed that far from spending the weekend with his wife, Captain Symonds had in fact spent it with Bennallack – whom he married four years after his wife 'disappeared' – in a country club in Cornwall.

Captain Symonds, he said, claimed his wife left him when they stopped in Plymouth, but the police contended that was completely out of character with Mrs Symonds, a loyal wife and mother who had been trying to keep the marriage alive. On the other hand, 10 days after Mrs Symonds supposedly walked out, Captain Symonds had moved Miss Bennallack into the marital home. Within a matter of weeks, his wife's property was being sold or given away – Captain Symonds, he said, must have known that his wife would never return, and known the reason why: he had murdered her and disposed of her body. He asked the jury to consider whether Captain Symonds' action indicated that his wife might have second thoughts and return, or whether it 'indicates a certainty that she had gone beyond recall.'

Mr Inskip also pointed out that just a year later in June, 1964, Freda and Symonds had a daughter. But it was not until he retired from the Army in 1966 that he started divorce proceedings on the grounds of desertion. Normally, papers have to be served on the respondent unless they are dead or cannot be found, so Symonds swore an affidavit in which he made three false statements: he said he had asked certain people if they knew the whereabouts of his wife, when in fact he had not; he swore that his wife had two brothers and a sister, but no knowledge of their whereabouts except that he believed one brother was in Canada; and he had said that he knew of no other relatives of whom enquiries could be made.

The divorce petition was filed in December, 1966, and in July the following year while serving in the Persian Gulf he swore another affidavit in which he said that his wife had left him in Plymouth saying that she was going to visit her sister, to which he replied: 'Oh, yes'. She took a small overnight bag from the car and left, never to be seen again.

If Captain Symonds was right, said Mr Inskip, this was a deliberate plan by his wife to desert him, but what was the need for such an elaborate plan when she could have walked out of the house on any day while he was working, and have taken her son with her?

He added that when Symonds had filed his petition, he had to admit his own adultery, but claimed that his relationship with Miss Bennallack had only begun after she moved into his house after his wife had deserted him: this was another lie.

He told the jury that over the past two years there had been considerable publicity about the disappearance of Mrs Symonds, whom he described as a quiet, kindly woman with an intense loyalty to her husband, yet there had not been a sound from her, despite the fact that her husband was on trial for her murder.

First to be called to the witness stand was Regimental Sergeant Major Edward Keay, who was with the 7th Royal Signals Regiment in Herford when Symonds and his wife were stationed there. He described Mrs Symonds as like 'a typical Girl Guide captain', serious but supportive of her husband in every way. Symonds, on the other hand, was not in the same mould: he was a flamboyant type, a man who was a great showman and a good actor.

He told the jury that Symonds caused a great deal of eyebrow-raising at a Christmas party when he turned up with Miss Bannallack instead of his wife – despite the fact that he and his wife had been invited, and not his escort.

Mr Keay's wife, Catherine, said she used to go on shopping expeditions with Doris – or Phill as she liked to be called – and when their son, Martin, was born, she showed no signs of being fed up. She was a very quiet, reserved person, but very reliable and dependable.

Expectant eyes turned to the witness box when Mr Leonard Phillips, the 58-year-old brother of Mrs Symonds, stepped in to give evidence, for it was he who had started what turned out to be a murder inquiry. A sales executive, he

WESTCOUNTRY WOODLAND … Does the body of Mrs Symonds still lie buried somewhere in Devon or Cornwall?

said that the Phillips family of father, mother and four children were not really close, but they did keep in touch. He recalled that he had given his sister away on her marriage on June 14, 1947. They visited him five years later when he was living at Iver and to all appearances seemed to be happy.

But since that time he had not seen or heard from his sister. In 1970 he started making more intensive inquiries at the Army Officers' Records Section at Stanmore, Middlesex; made telephone calls to Cornwall; sought help from the Salvation Army, and placed advertisements in the personal columns of national newspapers – all to no avail.

Being unable to trace her, he got in touch with the police. And that was when Proven Sharpe became very interested.

Evidence was given by Mrs Florence Newman, of Bromley, Kent, the elder sister of Doris, which showed that the sisters were close, writing to each other at least once a fortnight during the war, while Captain and Mrs Symonds went to live with her mother in Tottenham for a time after their marriage. After their mother's death, she spent three months with Doris at Tottenham before Doris eventually left to join her husband in Germany. After that, she received letters from her about once a month, with one particular letter written in 1960 sticking in her mind. 'It's happened at last,' declared the letter, 'and we're both very pleased,' said Doris, announcing she was pregnant.

But after that, she never received another letter from her, even when they moved back to England on leave. Asked Mr Inskip: 'Had there been an upset as a result of this leave?' Replied Mrs Newman 'I thought there was something to do with accommodation.'

Called to the stand, Mrs Dorothea Crabtree said she and her husband became friendly with the Symonds in Egypt in 1950 and continued their friendship when they were posted together to Catterick for two years. But there was one occasion when Mrs Symonds and her son appeared on their doorstep. She was upset, but did not say anything that indicated that she wanted her marriage to end. She told the court that the couple had a reconciliation and later Captain Symonds said he had reconciled with his wife for Martin's sake.

But in September 1963, Captain Symonds had written to her saying that his wife had left him.

Staff Sergeant Alexander Morris said that early in June of that year, Captain Symonds had asked him to use his Dormobile to move his son and his cot and clothing to a house in Abbotskerswell, where he was to spend the weekend while his parents were away. 'He said he was going with his wife to make it up. I don't think he was getting on too well with his missus. The impression I got was that he just wanted time with her by himself. He said they were going to Cornwall,' said the officer. He saw his senior officer the following week when he called a meeting of senior personnel and said his wife had left him and he expected them to support him: he did not want them running around the camp gossiping.

But two or three weeks later, he was again asked to use his Dormobile by Captain Symonds – this time to move Freda and her luggage from her parents' home in Liskeard to his home in Kingskerswell.

Housekeeper Mrs Nora Banski said that after the weekend, Captain Symonds told her that his wife had left to look after her sister, who was desperately ill, and asked her to continue looking after their son until other arrangements could be made. But two weeks later she turned up at the house to find a 'second Mrs Symonds' at the cottage, and it was obvious that she had been sleeping in the double bed with the captain. After the discovery, she was sacked.

Mrs Annie Mugford, a former neighbour, told the court that after Mrs Symonds 'left', Captain Symonds told her he would have to employ a housekeeper and would have to go to Freda in Cornwall. When she arrived, she was introduced as Mrs Symonds, a widow, whom he had met in Germany after her husband was killed in a motor accident. They discussed the similarity of names, with Captain Symonds saying he thought it was remarkable, while Mrs Mugford said she thought it was

ROYAL PARADE, PLYMOUTH … Did Doris Symonds simply vanish from here?

very peculiar. She noticed, too, that the second Mrs Symonds called him Guy.

Several other witnesses testified to the fact that Captain Symonds had told them that his wife had left, with some claiming that Captain Symonds had said he had returned home to find his wife's clothes missing, plus a quantity of money. He also claimed that she had left behind a number of bills which he had had to pay, and had sold some of her things and borrowed money to pay them.

On the third day of the trial, it was the turn of Detective Chief Superintendent Proven Sharpe to take the stand. He was the one who had doggedly tracked down every shred of evidence in an attempt to convince the jury that Captain Symonds was a brutal killer who should pay for his crime with a spell behind bars. If anyone had damning evidence, it had to be him.

He told the court that he interviewed Symonds on December 10, 1971, and asked him to describe his relationship with Doris during the first seven or eight years of their marriage. Symonds told him: 'Well, being honest and truthful, one day after we got married we both realised we had made a mistake. I wanted children, and she did not want any. I slept with her as a married man and had intercourse 10 times at the most.'

Asked if that meant he was saying they were incompatible from the outset, he replied: 'We jogged along and made the best of a bad job. We never had rows. We were both even-tempered; she was placid and never raised her voice.' And what was his reaction when he found his wife was pregnant? 'I am very fond of children. She did not want it. I had to get all the gear, cot, pram, nappies, the lot. She did not want to do it – she did not want the child.'

Chief Superintendent Sharpe said Symonds told him that they had matrimonial difficulties purely because of their son: she could not handle children, she could not pick them up and did not have 'the knack'.He admitted that when they left Germany he suggested to his wife that they should split up because he was getting fed up with putting on a false front. Doris said that if they did, she would send the boy to an orphanage, but he thought it was a dreadful idea. They stayed together, but he had already met Freda, who he claimed was a casual friend to begin with. When he returned to Germany, however, their friendship began to ripen and he concealed his relationship from his wife, with whom he tried a reconciliation.

In March, 1962, he said, when he was posted back to Britain and Denbury Camp, he mentioned to his wife that he and Freda had grown close and thought it was best if they stopped living together. He told Proven Sharpe that her reply was: 'You won't leave me – I'll cause trouble.'

Turning to the day that Doris disappeared, Captain Symonds told the detective that they had decided, on her suggestion, to go away to Cornwall for the weekend, leaving Martin with the home help. 'We went zooming over Dartmoor and turned off by the china clay pits to Plymouth. She said she wanted to go there. I had never been to Plymouth before in my life, except passing through to Liskeard. I stopped in a side street; it was near Royal Parade. She got out of the car. I think she was going shopping. I read a newspaper and I heard the backdoor click. I saw her leaning in and I thought she was putting shopping in. She said: 'I won't be a minute.' I looked around and saw that her night-case was gone. I waited for two hours and then drove off. I was livid. She just went, just like that.'

Although he said he telephoned the hospital, he admitted that he had not gone to the police but had gone to spend the weekend with Freda at a country club.

Questioned as to what action he had taken over his wife's disappearance, Symonds said: 'Nothing. I was bloody mad. I was not particularly worried about myself: it was the fact that she had left Martin. That blasted woman must have planned it. On the heads of my children, that is the truth, Superintendent. She said 'you won't leave me' – and looking back I presume she meant to leave me.'

On the following Tuesday, he said, he received a telephone call at the camp from his wife in which she said: 'I'm off.' When he asked : 'What about Martin?' she simply put the telephone down. A few days later, there was another call from her. She said: 'I'm off, and before I have finished with you, I'll cause you trouble.' and that is the last I heard from Phill.' Asked if he had heard from her since, he said: 'No. She went out of the blue and promised she was going to cause trouble.' Symonds said he thought she had gone to Australia because her brother was there, but it was only recently that he had found out that her brother lived in Canada.

Continuing his evidence on day five, Detective Chief Superintendent Proven Sharpe was asked to outline ways of disposing a body. Mr Comym said he had heard that Symonds used to go shark fishing in Cornwall – would it be possible to dispose a body that way? Proven Sharpe admitted that his enquiries into the case had extended to bodies washed up on the beaches around Devon and Cornwall, including bodies found in rivers and lakes. 'Any body found in the United Kingdom, either on the coast, in rivers, on the land or wherever since June, 1963, has been subject to enquiries by us and there is no information to suggest that any body is that of the missing woman,' admitted the police chief.

He had also followed up missing people files and said the police had exhumed a body in Brixham Cemetery after obtaining an order from the Home Office because the post mortem report had not made it clear what the cause of death was. Prompted, he added that the police had also made some 'exploratory' diggings around Cedar Cottage, Symonds' home, but there was no evidence that Mrs Symonds was buried there or near the cottage where other holes and cavities had been explored.

Proven Sharpe pointed out that there were 548 mineshafts on Dartmoor, half of which would not be entered: it was only possible to drive to about 20 of them, he said.

Under cross-examination, he agreed that his questioning of the suspect was 'very searching', but from first to the last Symonds had denied murdering his wife, although that was not specifically put to him. From his questioning, he said, however, the inference could be drawn that he felt something had happened to his wife and that Symonds had something to do with it. He also admitted that a grey Wolsley car owned by Symonds in 1963 had been traced to its present owner and subjected to intensive forensic examination, but showed nothing connected with the murder.

With the prosecution evidence complete, the defence counsel then submitted that there was not enough proof to convict Captain Symonds, that he had no case to answer, and that he should walk away a free man with not a stain on his character.

The defence counsel had spent most of the day in legal submissions to the judge, Mr Justice Bristow, with Mr Comym claiming that even if the jury convicted him on the 'evidence' so far, the Court of Criminal Appeal, the Appeal Court, would quash the conviction on the grounds that the conviction was unsafe and unsatisfactory. Replied the judge: 'I have come to a clear conclusion on this matter, and I think it is only right to everybody involved that I should state it at once.' There was, he said, insufficient evidence for the jury to convict Captain Symonds – all that had been put forward was circumstantial evidence, the prosecution had not been able to positively prove that Captain Symonds had murdered his wife; how he had killed her; nor what he might have done with the body.

'The evidence which is brought forward is evidence of a number of circumstances, many of which are in a high degree suspicious. If this case had gone to the jury, I would have had to direct the jury: You come to your conclusion upon the evidence, not upon suspicion; you are not entitled to speculate. You are fully entitled to use your own good sense in drawing inferences from the evidence that has been put before you.' He said he would recall the jury on the following Monday and direct them to find Captain Symonds not guilty of murdering his wife.

At the news, Captain Symonds was seen to pull a handkerchief out of his pocket. He appeared to be weeping. He shook hands with his defence counsel and then left the dock on £50 bail to return for the formal verdict.

As he left the Castle in a maroon Spitfire sports car, Mr Brabin told reporters that Captain Symonds had been in prison for 21 weeks for a crime he did not commit. 'This is his first day of freedom – he is overwhelmed and I do not think it has really sunk in,' he said.

Immediately after his formal three-minute court appearance on the following Monday, Captain Symonds, wearing a green sports jacket, fawn trousers and his Royal Corps of Signals tie, was whisked away in a hired car, but his solicitor said that he would almost certainly not be applying for compensation for the time he spent in prison. 'The only way is to bring an action for malicious prosecution. This would be extremely difficult. It is unlikely that an action will be brought,' said Mr

Brabin.

Of course, the story made headline news in all the national and regional daily newspaper, with claims that Captain Symonds had been paid thousands of pounds by one newspaper for his story, and one Sunday newspaper even put up a £10,000 reward for anyone who positively found Mrs Symonds. On March 2 of that year, it was claimed that a woman had signed the visitors' book in a Betws-y-Coed, North Wales guest house as: "Doris Irene Symonds, Newton Abbot, July 9, 1968" and had arrived with a Mr Angus Stoppart, staying four days in separate rooms, but nothing was proved.

Dozens of people tried to claim the money, but to this day it remains safe in the newspaper's bank.

But that was not the end of the story by a long way. Captain Symonds and his wife eventually bought Jeffrey's Stores at Mary Tavy, just outside of Tavistock, but in January 1975 he appeared before Exeter Crown Court to be declared a bankrupt, with debts of £6,967. He told the court that his affairs started to go wrong after he was accused of murdering his first wife. He said he had had to sell his North Devon home for £16,500 when it was worth £30,000, and although he bought his business for £25,000 his profits were eaten away by the high interest he was paying.

It was in November 1977 that Captain Symonds died at Tavistock Hospital at the age of 54, leaving a widow and three children.

But two years after his death, police were still investigating the case. In December 1979, Detective Superintendent Colin Moore, who worked on the case with Proven Sharpe, was following up a "dramatic clue" – 62 year old scrap dealer Mr Reg Matthews of East Ogwell, claimed to have found a patch of disturbed ground near the old army camp. Said the detective: 'We still get one or two leads on this case every year, and each one has to be checked out.'

Police eventually climbed down a narrow cavern near Newton Abbot to investigate Mr Matthews 'claim that the body might be buried under three feet of earth and rock. He said he had reported the grave to the police years before, but they had never investigated it. 'It looked as if the ground had been prepared for a body – it was not the work of children – but I do not think I was taken seriously,' he said as the police team prepared to dig. After digging for more than an hour, police announced that they had found nothing but a few pieces of wood.

The mystery remains: what happened to Doris Symonds? Was she murdered, or did she simply just vanish?

STRANGE ANIMALS

STORIES of some strange large cat stalking the rolling hills of Exmoor, taking sheep and lambs and leaving little or no trace of what exactly it is, seem to have been with us for generations.

But the fact is, the black beast of Exmoor did not start off as an Exmoor phenomenon: it began life in the Tedburn St Mary area, near Exeter, in April 1970 when two people – a farmer's wife and a 14-year-old boy – reported a black mystery animal 'something like a panther' to the police. A week later, police at Plympton were investigating a report from an Effordleigh man who said he had seen a strange black animal near his home.

Plymouth at that time had a zoo run by Plymouth City Council and Chipperfield's Circus, and the first thing the police did was to inquire if one of their animals had gone missing. It had not.

Described as 'a large black creature, twice the size of a Labrador, with a small head and thick hind and forelegs,' the man spotted the beast from his greenhouse together with two friends.

Over the next few years, numerous sightings of the beast were made in Devon, but then the centre of operations changed, as if the creature had at last found the sort of countryside it really wanted – the wild open space of Exmoor. It was there that the legend took root and grew as its depredations struck something akin to fear into the families who eke out their living on the rolling, wind-blown hills. The Beast of Exmoor had been born.

It made headlines around the world and attracted big game hunters, farmers armed with shotguns and hounds, and even a troop of Royal Marines. But none of them have yet taken home a really clear photograph, let alone a head as a trophy for the living room wall. The beast is always one step ahead.

It was the voracity of its appetite which shocked people. Over 100 rams and lambs were devoured on one farm alone at South Molton at the rate or one, and sometimes two, a night.

Dozens of theories as to what the creature might be were put forward: a rogue lurcher dog, bred by poachers to hunt the moorland red deer; an escaped puma, or one that had been turned out of a private collection; a stray panther; a beast from the 'old days' which somehow survived into modern times; and even claims by one man that it was a werewolf stalking the hundreds of square miles of wild uninhabited upland heather and gorse moors bordered by the rugged and wooded North Devon and Somerset coastline.

The area the beast covered ranged from South Molton to Simonsbath, from Brayford to Hunters Inn, and in a land built for legend it did not take long for the Beast of Exmoor to turn into something like folklore – with a little more solid form. For this animal has defied modern technology, expert hunters and so-called experts with high velocity rifles equipped with night-sights.

While everyone knows that wild boars, bears and wolves at one time roamed the forests of Britain, no one believed that such a creature could secretly exist in our crowded island. And when it was established that there was some mysterious beast attacking animals in the dead of night and leaving their half-eaten carcases as positive evidence of its existence, it created a furore of interest.

But no matter how hard people hunted for the beast, or family of beasts, it was not one to hang around and be caught. Lures, traps, hidden cameras, people waiting up all night at likely places with fingers poised on hair-triggers meant nothing to it. In fact, it was almost as if the beast could smell or sense that something strange was going on in its territory.

One of the most tenacious of the beast hunters has been author and naturalist Trevor Beer, who has also written numerous books

STALKING THE COUNTRYSIDE … A puma-like creature could still roam the moors and woods of the West.

and articles on the mystery animal. 'I had always felt that the occasional reports of sheep killing on Exmoor, and indeed anywhere else, was likely to have been caused by rogue dogs. It was not until the mass killing in the area of Drewstone that my passing interest became kindled into burning curiosity,' he was reported as saying.

'I wanted to know exactly what could kill 80 sheep in only 90 days or so in one small area of Exmoor. I was asked to see if I could help track the animal which everyone was calling The Beast.'

After joining the posse – which included huntsmen with their dogs, police and a huge group of angry and bewildered local farmers – he became the first person to photograph a kill. 'Sherlock Holmes would have paled at the lack of clues,' said Mr Beer. 'I decided to poke around and get the lie of the land The Beast was using as a larder. Patchwork quilted fields overlooked a steep valley side clothed with conifer plantations and in the valley bottom the track of a disused railway was an ideal corridor between farms. From the noise, the shouting, the blowing of horns, the baying of hounds and movements of the horses there was no way any self-respecting beast would hang around to get caught,' he told a local newspaper reporter. And he was right, of course: no one saw anything.

Together with another local naturalist, Nigel Brierley, who believed that a large number of feral cats – possibly some mutants among them which had bred and evolved over scores of years to a size large enough to bring down and kill a sheep – were roaming the hills and dales, they began an in-depth investigation of every clue which came their way. But the trail ran cold until one day Mr Beer was telephoned and asked if there was such a thing as an elephant's graveyard for red deer. His reply, of course, was negative. So why, he was asked, were there so many red deer corpses in this one place?

The trouble was, the 'graveyard' was nowhere near Exmoor – it was closer to Exeter. In a woodland he found one fully grown hind with its throat ripped out. Nearby he found a dozen similar carcasses. Not unnaturally, Trevor set up a watch and noticed

PERFECT COVER … Who can be sure what lurks in such remote places?

69

that the deer visited a certain stream to drink. Walking up the stream one day, he looked up into the bushes and noticed the head and shoulders of a large animal appear out of the bushes. Said Mr Beer afterwards: 'In the green sundappled shadows of the wood, it looked black and rather like an otter, a first impression I shall always remember for the head was broad and sleek with small ears. The animal's eyes were clear greeny yellow as I just stood still and stared at it.

'As it stared back at me, I could clearly make out the thickish neck, the powerful-looking forelegs and deep chest. Then, without a sound, it turned and moved swiftly away through the trees. That it was jet black I was sure, and the long body and tail I guessed at four-and-a-half-feet in length and about two feet at the shoulders. I had dropped my camera bag at the bushes where it appeared. Reaching the wood edge I could see the animal already two thirds of the way across the adjoining field and moving at great speed. It ran like a greyhound, its forelegs pushing through the hind legs which seemed to go forward in front of its round head as it raced away. A beautiful, very large black panther was my immediate thought. I watched it reach the field edge where it leapt high into the hedge and disappeared. I never saw it again.'

But a lot of other people did. Like a Mrs Cooper of Merton, who claims she saw a stone-coloured puma twice between North Molton and South Molton and between West Buckland and South Molton. And what was reported as a lioness was seen near Littleham, near Bideford, and later near Fairy Cross and Parkham. Later, a fawn coloured puma was spotted in the area between Eggesford to Kings Nympton, Muddiford to Braunton and again near Bideford and Umberleigh. In fact, so many were reported from the moorland area between Knowstone and Morchard Bishop that the district became known as Cat Moor.

Clearly, says Trevor, more than one big cat is at large in the area, for although big cats travel quite a distance – their territories in the wild can extend for up to 100 miles – the number of sightings and their timings make it impossible for it to be just one animal. And one self-confessed poacher told him in hushed tones:

A GLIMPSE … the beast's eyes shone yellow in the beam of the lamp.

'You're looking for a black panther. I saw it on the River Barle between Simonsbath and Challacombe. He soon made off when

I put the light on him.'

Says Trevor: 'One thing I feel positive about is that all the eye-witnesses are not suffering from hallucinations – the vast majority of sightings are real enough.' And that includes his own, of course!

But what positive evidence is there for the existence of a big cat? Plaster casts taken of footprints have turned out to be those of a large dog, and for some strange reason no one has ever been able to photograph the animal, or animals. But Trevor is adamant that there are some big cats prowling Exmoor, possibly ones which have escaped or been deliberately freed and have since hybridised under the conditions.

Certainly Cornish zoologist Dr Frank Turk, of Camborne, would agree with him. He told a newspaper in January 1985 that he had found hairs on bramble bushes in Surrey – another great puma rumour area – which could only have come from one of the large cat family.

A former reader in Natural History at Exeter University, he examined hairs through a microscope and performed a series of exhaustive tests before satisfying himself that they belonged to the puma family. 'Puma hairs are quite distinctive,' he told a reporter from the *Western Morning News*, 'and I am absolutely certain these animals are living wild in Britain. I think pumas are responsible for killing the sheep. They probably escaped or were released from small private zoos and are now breeding successfully. Pumas are usually quite amenable to humans – there have been only four incidents in the past 150 years of pumas attacking a human. Pumas have wide hunting areas and can easily travel up to 100 miles.'

The hairs examined by Dr Turk were supplied by naturalist Di Francis of Torquay, who has spent years trying to prove her theory that a big cat survived the Ice Age in Britain.

If so, that could account for the hundreds of other sightings of a black cat in various parts of the country – not just on Exmoor. There have been sightings of big cats in Surrey, Wales, the Isle of Wight, the Sussex border, many other parts of Devon and even as far west as Penzance. In fact, only two days after Dr Turk had

DARTMOOR ... A wilderness remaining largely unchanged today.

asserted that big cats were alive and well and living in the South West, retired builder Sydney Bowder and his wife Violet reported watching one from the window of their cottage at Goonlaze, where they had lived for more than 50 years.

'We often see foxes. But this was bigger – it looked like an oversized cat,' said Mr Bowden. 'We are used to seeing all sorts of wild animals, but we have never seen anything like this. It looked something like a cat, but it was much bigger than any cat I have ever seen.' And just a few days later, farmer Gordon Phillips, aged 71, reported a puma crossing his yard at Bridge, near Redruth. 'Part of its tail was missing and it was not looking in very good condition,' said Mr Phillips, who added that the animal ran off towards the village. 'As a farmer, you get used to looking at animals and judging their condition. The cat looked hollow and as if it didn't have many days left,' he said. But no one ever found a body. A short time later, however, a puma-like animal was reported on a farm near St Stephens in mid-Cornwall, but a few days later it – or a relative – was back on Exmoor.

'I could have touched it,' declared Mrs Jill Yendell, who said she was driving near Rackenford with a mini-bus full of children when The Beast appeared. 'It came out of the woods in front of us. It had a long tail, a puma-like head, pricked ears and a grey body. It looked very weathered as it bounded across the country lane. It jumped across the road in two bounds and was gone,' said Mrs Yendell, of Witheridge.

The legend of the beast took another turn in December 1985 with speculation after a paw print was found at Woodcombe Farm, near Minehead. It followed the reported 'theft' of 20lb of tripe from at outhouse owned by 38-year-old Mrs Brenda Cornish, who farmed a smallholding. A national newspaper claimed that the beast was in fact an American wolverine and produced a photograph of the paw print to prove it. Unfortunately, the story had one vital flaw – the picture showed only four toes … and a wolverine has five!

'A jet-black cat resembling a panther has been spotted at County Gate on the northern coast of Exmoor. It was seen slinking through dead bracken four miles from Lynton around the Devon-Somerset border …' So begins another tale of The Beast, this time reported by Mrs Kezia Sandford and her husband, of Bay View Road, Woolacombe. 'We were parked at County Gate waiting for the start of an organised walk. I saw the animal on a grass clearing about 60 yards away. It was slightly shorter than an Alsatian, jet black with a long, lean body and a long tail. It was an agile mover. It seemed wary and ran by us to a stream at the bottom of the hill. It certainly didn't look like any breed of dog we know,' she said.

'An awful snarling howl that has startled and upset residents between Buryas Bridge and Sancreed in Cornwall may mean Penwith is once again being stalked by a mysterious predator. It has been over a year since sightings of the Morvah Cat and similar 'puma-like' beasts have been reported, but an unnerving encounter on a dark January night may have altered that,' said a

BODMIN MOOR … Another reputed haunt of the Beast.

report in *The Cornishman* at Penzance in January 1992.

It was a report of another encounter with the strange beast of the night which has been terrorizing the Westcountry, and this time was confronted by Richmond Heywood, who lives with his wife near the Buryas Bridge Garage, which he owns. On the main Land's End road, it is set in a valley which is surrounded by a mixture of woods, meadows and thick scrub – just the territory The Beast likes to camouflage itself in.

Locking up the garage one night, in the corner of a field he heard a sound that made his scalp creep. Something big was thrashing about and 'squealing like a pig being slaughtered'. As he peered into the darkness trying to make out what it was, the noise started towards him … and then stopped. Suddenly, the still night was rent by a loud growl and a howl. Mr Heywood reports that he explored no further but hastened home to tell his wife. The next morning, however, he returned to the scene but

AN OLD ENGRAVING … Dartmoor has always retained its mysteries.

was unable to find any signs of a struggle or any blood.

His wife, he said, now insists that he takes a stout stick with him whenever he is alone at the garage, and since the incident Mr Heywood says he has been approached by several friends and acquaintances from as far afield as Sancreed who have told him stories of strange encounters with beasts which made noises in the night.

Having lived in the countryside for many years, he says he is familiar with the often eerie noises made by foxes and badgers, but was convinced that the noise he heard was of a small pig being killed by a larger animal.

Over the years, dogs have been blamed for a great many sheep killings, and there is no doubt that in many cases they have been the culprits. In packs, they become savage beasts with a wolf-like blood lust. In April 1992 dogs were being blamed for a number of sheep killings on Bodmin Moor, although local farmers were adamant that it was the work of a big cat.

Rosemary Rhodes, who farms 25 acres at Ninestones Farm, Commonmoor, near Bolventor, lost six sheep in less than four months – most killed in daylight – and claims that one was found 'with the entire contents of her rib cage eaten out. Every bone on her rib cage was boned out better than a butcher would do, and her two front legs were missing. It is very strange. Only one attacked sheep has been found alive. It was a fat ewe which had rip marks all down her stomach and something had half eaten its back leg.

'The wounds were four, side by side, half an inch apart, about four inches long, straight as though they were done with a sharp knife. Whatever had done it had gone through the skin, but dogs don't do that,' reported Mrs Rhodes, who had farmed at Ninestones for four years.

'I could see the wounds went right through the abdominal wall and no dog has claws that long or teeth sharp enough to do that. I was told by the slaughterman that this ewe was definitely not killed by dogs, and that gave me the courage to report the matter to the Ministry.'

Fifty-three-year-old Mrs Rhodes took the sheep to a local abattoir where slaughtermen finished off the still living animal and agreed that the wounds were not made by dogs, but a Ministry of Agricultural veterinary expert, who examined the carcass, insisted that the sheep had been attacked by dogs.

Mrs Rhodes, however, took two plaster casts of the beast's footprints and believed that its lair was in privately owned forest overlooking her land.

Farm hand Don Rogers vehemently denied that it was a dog which confronted him in the night, with its yellow eyes glowing in the light of his lamp, as he went to check the sheep on the farm. 'It stopped dead in the light and stared at me for a minute, with its yellow eyes glowing, then it turned and went off very quickly,' said 33-year-old Mr Rogers, of Redgate, near St Cleer.

'I'm used to seeing animals' eyes in the beam of my lamp, and I've never seen an animal with eyes that shine yellow. I don't mind admitting that it sure as hell frightened me. I'll never forget it.

'It was dark brown and grey and its body was about four feet long. It stood about three feet high and by its speed and stride it had to be a cat-like animal. I know what I saw, and nothing can change that.'

He added: 'I'm not afraid of dogs, foxes, or any other animal on the moor, but I've not been out rabbiting at night since I saw that thing.'

Beast hunter Nigel Brierley, who has been on the trail of the big cat for at least 10 years with Trevor Beer, claimed that a second eye-witness had shot at the animal on Bodmin Moor, as it was sitting on a stone wall, but had missed. And he also claimed that a retired farmer at Luxulyan, near St Austell, had sighted what must have been a puma.

His own book has a photograph of a puma on the front cover, which he says was taken in Cornwall. 'We really think the beast is a puma' he told the *Cornish Guardian*. 'It seems more than probably from the reports we have received and from the evidence gathered by a tracker who went to Bodmin Moor to investigate the case. He discovered pad marks about four inches across which are definitely those of a puma.'

Although he refused to disclose the tracker's identity – because he shuns publicity – 72-year-old Mr Brierley added: 'There are pumas on the loose in Devon and Cornwall, but it is very difficult to get the powers that be to take the situation seriously. On our side of Exmoor, we have no doubt that there are pumas around. The farmers know it, but the authorities do not accept it.'

Whatever is causing the sheep, deer and other animal deaths is still a baffling mystery, despite the intensive hunts which have been made. And it looks set to remain so for the forseeable future until one of the beasts is caught, alive or dead.

But the biggest question is: Could there be an animal in the United Kingdom which has secretly survived the Ice Age?

MOORLAND FRINGE ... Will countryside such as this ever give up the secret of the Beast?

GOING OFF THE RAILS

THE one thing about ghosts that make them creepy is their uncanny silence. Very few spectres bother to talk to we mortals as they perambulate their domain. Perhaps we are not worth bothering with – or perhaps *we* are the ghosts to them.

One Westcountry ghost would find it exceedingly difficult to communicate with us – for it happens to be a train!

This train runs between Washford and Watchet in Somerset, on the track of the West Somerset Mineral Railway. Not only do people claim to have seen the phantom train, but they also say they have heard the ringing voices of children from the turn of the century as they return from their holiday at Minehead.

Reports are that the train was a tank engine, like many which ran on the minor lines in the South West in the last years of Queen Victoria, and while claims of the train's existence can be traced back from 1901 to the First World War, it was only when the line was closed in 1917 and the rails torn up to be sent to make into war weapons, that the first of a whole string of sightings started.

According to records, a bad incident occured on the line at Kentsford on August 22, 1857 when an engine left Roadwater with a truck carrying 30 labourers home to Watchet. At Washford, crossing keeper Henry Giles stepped out onto the line waving his flag for the train to stop. He warned the driver not to go any further because a coal train was expected shortly from Watchet.

But assistant engineer John James, riding on the footplate, said

GHOST TRAIN ... Manifestations of phantom trains have been reported by reliable witnesses in the South West.

he had to get to town urgently as he had letters to post: he decided to go on. With Henry Giles riding on the buffer beam, the train continued at 20mph, whistling all the time as a warning.

But as the train rounded a bend at Kentsfold, the coal train was approaching them about 200 yards away. Both engine drivers applied their brakes, but there was a sound of tortured metal as the engines collided head-on. Giles died instantly and James and another man died of their wounds later. Many others were injured and scalded as the boiler of one of the trains exploded.

According to reports in the *Taunton Chronicle* of August 26 and September 2, 1857, the coroner recorded a verdict of manslaughter against James after the three-day hearing. What is odd about the story is that it was nearly 50 years before the ghost train made its first journey. Local people claim to have heard the sound of the train approaching, whistle blowing, while others say they have heard the screams of wounded passengers. Some claim to have seen the light of the fire as the stoker shovelled in coal to keep the train at a steady speed.

What is curious is the fact that the train runs on rails which are no longer there! And curious also is the fact that some of the reports speak of ghost children's voices when the people involved were all tough male labourers.

If the ghost train is heard and seen nowadays, people are keeping quiet about their experiences, but just after the Second World War a local postman and his friend decided to investigate the story. The pair had been to band practice, and on their way home they were about to cross over the bridge near the brickworks when they saw a train silently coming towards them drawing a line of trucks. As it reached the bridge, it disappeared.

At first, they kept quiet about their experience, but later told a local journalist – it became headline news. And then other people braved public scorn and came forward to tell of their encounters.

The two men faced a barrage of laughter, but one person took their claims seriously. He was interested in the occult and convinced that they were telling the truth, he, too, went in search of the phantom train. For two nights nothing happened, but on the third night all three set out to keep watch.

They were about to give up when one of them gave a shout and pointed down the line – approaching was the distinct image of a tank engine travelling at about 20mph. It continued on its course and just as the two men had said, vanished as soon as it had passed under the bridge. But unlike many other people who claimed to have seen the train, they heard no sound at all.

Convinced of what they had seen, all three swore affidavits with a local solicitor and once again the train became front page news.

In the years since then, however, the train has not only remained silent but mysteriously invisible.

THE
VANISHING LANDS

LEGENDS of lost lands are legion – one only has to think of the lost city of Atlantis and the plethora of stories which have been told down the centuries about its people – and probably the most famous 'missing country' in the South West is Lyonesse, that land which lies between Land's End and the Scilly Isles.

Tales of bold knights of old fighting in a green and verdant land as they hunt for the Holy Grail have been told since storytelling was invented. Whether any of them are true is pure conjecture, but is there any substance to the story of Lyonesse lying submerged beneath the tidal race which sweeps around the tip of the foot of England? There might be.

Standing on Land's End and looking out to the Scilly Isles on the other side of one of the most dangerous channels around the coast of Britain, it is hard to imagine that expanse covered with a land which vanished – so it is said – within historic times. At one time, according to old stories, the land of Lyonesse linked Cornwall to the Scillies.

Inhabited by the Silures, Lyonesse – sometimes called Lethowsow – residents were supposedly noted for their hard work and their religious fervour. Their piety can be judged from the fact that according to *Polwhele's History of Cornwall* it was unbelievable. Reporting the story of the flood which overtook the land, this noted Cornish historian says: 'The number of parish churches lost is so astonishingly great as to baffle the powers of evidence, to preclude the possibility of conviction. I,

FLEEING FROM THE WAVES ... The engulfing sea pursues a Trevilian horseman.

therefore, take it upon me to reduce the number from 140 to 40 – to cut off what any dash of Worcester's pen might casually created, the first figure.' Polwhele, then, was taking his information from *The Chronicle of Florence Worcester*, originally written in 1490 and translated by Thomas Forester and published in 1834. She in turn was quoting from *The Saxon Chronicle* when she declared: 'On the third of the Nones of November (1099) the sea overflowed the shore, destroying towns and drowning many persons and innumerable oxen and sheep.'

Chronicler Robert Hunt towards the end of the last century claimed that the Seven Stones Reef was said to mark the place where a large city had once stood, but his research led him to believe that the land vanished over a comparatively long period instead of by a 'great cataclysm'. There is, he admits in *Popular Romances of the West of England*, only one hint to this viewpoint. 'One of the ancestors of the Trevilians is said to have had time to remove his family and his cattle; but at last he had to fly himself with all the speed which a fleet horse could give him.'

From this, he says, it might appear that although the catastrophe was gradual at first, the waters, having once broken through any sea defences which might have been in existence, then became a raging torrent which burst over the area in an uncontrolled fury. 'By this war of waters, several large towns were destroyed, and an immense number of the inhabitants perished,' says Mr Hunt.

He adds that at one time a small but very ancient oratory, called Chapel Idne or the Narrow Chapel once stood in Sennen Cove. It was allegedly paid for by a Lord of Goonhilly, who owned a portion of land in Lyonesse, in praise of his own escape from the destruction which overtook his bretheren.

Davies Gilbert takes the Trevilian story a stage further in his book, *The Parochial History of Cornwall*, but states that the man's surname was actually Trevelyan. 'A cave is pointed out in Perranuthnoe, where the ancestor of the Trevelyans is said to have been borne on shore, by the strength of his horse, from the destructions of the Lionesse (*sic*) country west of the Land's End. The Trevelyan family are too old, too honourable, and now too much distinguished by science, for them to covet any addition of honour through the medium of fabulous history,' he says.

A little more is added by Drew and Hitchin's in their book on Cornwall: 'One of the family of Trevilian, now residing in Somerset, but originally Cornish, saved himself by the assistance of his horse at the time of this inundation; and it is reported that the arms of this family were taken from this fortunate escape, to commemorate his providential preservation,' it is claimed. Another tidbit of information on this miracle escape is added by another Cornish researcher, who says that the coat of arms 'bears gules a horse argent, from a less wavy argent, and azure, issuing out of a sea proper.'

Davies Gilbert, a well-respected Cornish historian, continues the tale by adding that after the destruction of the legendary land 'men remembered not the like to have ever happened before,' adding that 'and the same day was the first of the new moon.' No one is quite sure what the significance of this was!

He also points out that Stow, who wrote his History of England in 1580, notices the cataclysm of 1099 when he said: 'The sea brake in over the banks of the Thames and other ryvers, drowning many towns and much people, with innumerable numbers of oxen and sheepe; at which time the lands of Kent, that sometime belonged to the Duke of Godwyne, Earle of Kent, were covered with sandes and drowned, which are to this day called the Godwyne Sandes.'

Davies Gilbert concludes that Florence of Worcester either invented – 'or, with monkish credulity' – received the tale that a whole district was engulfed at Land's End, not in some geologically distant time, but in what may be regarded as a recent authentic period of history. This, he says, was at a time when systematic registers were being compiled and an event which must have shaken the whole of Europe appears to go unrecorded.

'To increase the wonder,' he says, 'a gentleman, accidentally on horseback, is carried by this animal to the neighbouring shore of Whitsand Bay, or twenty miles further off, to Perranuthnoe, through a sea which had swallowed an entire country, and from

SEEKER AFTER TRUTH ... a visitor looks out towards the lost land of Lyonesse.

which the largest modern vessels could not possibly have escaped. This idle tale, related by one writer after another, has almost reached our own times,' he says. And, of course, it has!

He adds he remembered one female relative of a former Vicar of St Erth who had a dream in which she was instructed to prepare various decotations of herbs and, standing on Land's End, was to pour them into the sea with certain incantations. This done, the mysterious lost land of Lyonesse would rise from the depths of the sea, complete with all its inhabitants still alive.

Perchance some form was unobserved,

Perchance in prayer or faith she swerved

says Mr Gilbert, adding: 'No country appeared, and although the love of marvellous events, and of tales exciting the passions, seems not to have diminished in recent times, yet the editor is unaware of any subsequent attempt having been made to rescue those unfortunate people from their protracted state of suspended animation.'

FOLLOWING A DREAM … Trying to raise Lyonesse with herbs and incantations.

'Although a sweep of ocean, twenty-seven miles in breadth, separates at present the Land's End from the Scilly Islands, there can yet be little doubt of their having been heretofore united to each other by the mainland,' asserts the Rev Richard Warner in his book, *A Tour through Cornwall in the Autumn of 1808.*

'The records of history indeed do not rise so high as the era when this disjunction was first effected; but we have documents yet remaining which prove to us that this strait must have been considerably widened, and that the number of Scilly Islands greatly increased within the last sixteen or seventeen centuries, by the waters of the Atlantic (receding probably from the coast of America) pressing towards this coast of Britain, accumulating upon Bolerium, and overwhelming part of the western shores of Cornwall,' he goes on.

The worthy vicar then says that at the time of the Phoenicians when Cornwall was referred to as the Cassiterides – from the Greek for tin – there were only ten islands in the Scillies, but there are now one hundred and forty rocky islets. Oddly enough, that's exactly the number of churches which were supposed to have vanished!

William of Worcester, continues the vicar, wrote 'with a degree of positive exactitude, stamping authority upon its recital' that between Mount's Bay and the Scilly Islands there had previously been woods, meadows and arable land. Incredulously, he goes on to say: 'Uninterrupted tradition since this period, which subsists to the present day vigorous and particular, authenticates his account, and leaves no doubt upon the mind that a vast track of land, which stretched anciently from the eastern shores of Mount's Bay to the north-western rock of Scilly (with the exception of the narrow strait flowing between the Longships and Land's End) has, since the age of Strabo and Solinus, and previous to that of William of Worcester, been overwhelmed and usurped by the waves of the sea.' He almost makes out that it must be true because people say so – even when writing thirteen centuries after the event, as William of Worcester did.

Interestingly, he adds the depths of water between Land's

THE HOAR ROCK ... An old engraving of St Michael's before the castle was built.

End and the Scillies, claiming that at Land's End it is about eleven fathoms; at the Longships about eight; to the north, twenty, and fifteen between them and the north-west of Scilly. The shallowest point is midway between Cornwall and the Scilly Islands, he says.

William Borlase draws on the alleged inundation for evidence that Mount's Bay was once wooded, and that the Mount once stood proud of these lands. What gave credence to his report was his first-hand account of having seen tree stumps in Mount's Bay at extremely low tides. He adds that the shallow flats between the present islands of Scilly, which are dry at low tide in many instances, are also evidence that the islands themselves were linked at one time.

'The flats between Trescaw (Tresco), Brehar (Bryher) and

Sampson are quite dry at a spring-tide, and men easily pass dry-shod from one island to another over sandbanks (where upon the shifting of the sands, walls and ruins are frequently discovered) upon which, at full sea, there are ten and twelve feet of water,' he says in *An Account of the Great Alteration which the Islands of Scylley have Undergone*. Psychic dowsers Paul Broadhurst and Hamish Miller have detected a powerful energy line at Land's End while tracing the St Michael ley line. It points towards the Scilly Isles, they both claim in their book *The Sun and the Serpent* and at Carn Les Boel there is a powerful force at work. 'What we found at this spot is inexplicable,' they say.

References to St Michael's Mount standing proud in a wood are also legion. Of course, its Titanic origin – myth has it that it was formed by two giants, one from Brittany and the other from Cornwall, throwing rocks at one another from opposite sides of the English Channel, or that Cormoran, the Cornish giant, built it when he kicked a rock out of his wife's apron in a temper – is more than a little doubtful, but its old Cornish name, 'Careg-lus en kuz' means 'The white rock in the wood.'

According to historian Leland in his *Itinerary*: 'A forest is supposed to have extended along the coast to St Michael's Mount, which was described as a 'hoare rock in a wood' and stood five or six miles in extent, formed into parishes, each having its church, and laid out in meadows, cornfields and woods.' Another investigator claims that the previous name of the Mount was Careg-Cawse, or the Gray Rock – in Saxon it is 'Mychelyroz', or Michael's Place.

Just along the coast from the Mount is an anchorage known as Gwavas Lake. Robert Hunt claims it is 'not a little curious' that what is now the sea should be called a lake, but the tradition that a beech wood extended right across Mount's Bay would explain the situation – it would at one time have been an inland lake. By its side, he says, a saint lived in a hermitage and he was celebrated far and wide for his holiness and his ability to cure people of all sorts of ailments, both of the body and soul. 'None ever came in the true spirit who failed to find relief. The prayers of the saint and the waters of the lake removed the severest pains from the limbs and the deepest sorrows from the mind. The young were strengthened and the old revived by their influences,' he says.

What happened was that the 'Great Flood' which swept away Lyonesse submerged the forest and then destroyed the lands 'of this lovely and almost holy lake, burying beneath the waters church and houses, and destroying alike the people and the priest.' Those who survived the catastrophe built a church on the hill and dedicated it to the saint of the lake – St Pol – which is now modernised into St Paul, adds Mr Hunt.

Supporting his claim for the area to have once been heavily wooded, he goes on to say that he has heard that the parish records of St Paul note that tithes were collected from lands which have disappeared, and then adds his own experience as a footnote: 'I have passed in a boat from St Michael's Mount to Penzance on a summer day, when the waters were very clear, and the tide low, and seen the black masses of trees in the white sands extending far out into the bay.

'On one occasion, when I was at school in Penzance, after a violent equinoctial gale, large trunks of trees were thrown up on the shore, just beyond Chyandour, and then with the other boys I went, at the lowest of the tide, far out over the sands and saw scores of trees embedded in the sands. We gathered nuts – they were beech-nuts – and leaves in abundance. It is not a little remarkable – if it be true, as I am informed it is – that the trees found in the Pentuan Stream Works, under some fifty or sixty feet of sand and silt, are beech-trees, and that they were destroyed when the fruit was upon them.'

The one really puzzling point of all this 'evidence' is the date of this catastrophe – 1099. *The Domesday Book* was compiled just after the Norman Conquest of 1066 – in 1086, in fact – and makes no mention at all of Lyonesse! As this was the most complete register of land in the British Isles ever written, when every acre was recorded, and to whom it belonged or was farmed, it seems strange that its compilers should miss such a large chunk of land, measuring some twenty-two miles long by

LOST LANDS … Does Lyonesse lie beneath this beautiful sea?

several miles wide. As it happens, however, modern scholars have been unable to find three manors mentioned as having been in Cornwall at the time – but they are not large enough to account for the acreage which would have existed between Land's End and the Scilly Isles – and in any event the 'missing manors' are not in Penwith, or Connerton as it was then.

Could the event have been much earlier? After all, the first record of the land's disappearance was not written until some time later – and oral tradition has a way of being embroidered!

We have evidence of Latin author Diodorus Siculous writing in the first century of the Christian era who, when describing tin streaming in Cornwall, refers to the island of Ictis, where 'during the ebb of the tide, the ground between is left dry, and they carry over to the island the tin in abundance in their waggons.'

This in itself would indicate that St Michael's Mount was already an island long before the Norman invasion – it would be quite incredible if Siculous could invent history before it happened!

And we also have stories of a mysterious land and city on the North Cornwall coast near Newquay. 'We cannot say how many years since, but once there stood on the northern shores of Cornwall, extending over all that country between the Gannel and Perranporth, a large city called Langarrow or Langona,' says Mr Hunt, who adds that the sandhills of the district now cover the city but 'the memory of the sad and sudden catastrophe still lingers among the peasantry.'

The tradition, he says, always mentioned that the city disappeared 900 years ago and that in its prime it was the largest in England with seven churches, which were remarkable for their beauty and size. 'The inhabitants were wealthy, and according to received accounts, they drew their wealth from a large tract of level land thickly wooded in some parts, and highly cultivated in others – from the sea, which was overflowing with fish of all kinds – and from mines, which yielded them abundance of tin and lead,' says Mr Hunt.

He adds that criminals were transported from other parts of Britain to work on the mines on the coast and were also employed in constructing a new harbour in the Gannel and clearing it of sand so that large ships could tie up and take away the produce.

'This portion of the population of Langarrow,' he continues, 'were not allowed to dwell within the city. The convicts and their families had to construct huts or dig caves on the wild moors of this unsheltered northern shore, and to this day evidences of their existence are found under the sands, in heaps of wood-ashes, amidst which are discovered considerable quantities of mussel and cockle shells, which we may suppose was their principal food.'

Flourishing for a long time, 'sin, in many of its worst forms, was however present amongst the people – the convicts sent to Langarrow were of the vilest. They were long kept widely sepa-

rated, but use breeds familiarity, and gradually the more design-
ing of the convicts persuaded their masters to employ them
within the city. The result of this was, after a few years, an amal-
gamation of the two classes of the population. The daughters of
Langarrow were married to the criminals, and thus crime
became the familiar spirit of the place. The progress of this may
have been slow – the result was, however, sure: and eventually,
when vice was dominant, and the whole of the population sunk
in sensual pleasures, the anger of the Lord fell upon them.'

According to the story, a violent storm blew up, running for
three days and nights. During that time, the sandhills which run
from Crantock to Perran were formed, burying the city, its
churches, the houses and its inhabitants in a common grave.
Comments Mr Hunt: 'To the present time those sandhills stand
a monument to God's wrath; and in several places we certainly
find considerable quantities of bleached human bones, which
are to many strong evidence of the correctness of tradition.'

Well, it certainly sounds as if Mr Hunt believed in a Sodom
and Gomorrah way of putting things right!

But the fact is, it is not impossible for there to have been dry
land stretching out from the present-day Cornwall, or for it to
have vanished over the centuries. In April 1990, geophycisists at
a Plymouth conference were told that an earthquake a day hit
Britain on average – with the second biggest in the past one
hundred years only two weeks before. It registered just over 5
on the Richter scale and its epicentre was near the village of
Clun, near Shrewsbury in Shropshire, but its effects were felt as
far away as Exeter and Barnstaple. Said scientist David
Redmayne at the time: 'We would not normally expect that size
of earthquake in Britain more than four times a century. We had
one slightly bigger in 1984 and to get two that size in six years is
quite exceptional.' However, eleven people have been killed in
British earthquakes between 1580 and 1940.

The fact is, the April earthquake broke windows in a Seaton,
Devon, office and shook offices in Exeter. Police received calls
from all over the region, claiming: 'It must have been sizeable
for us to have felt it down here.'

Cornwall and parts of Devon lie across a geological fault line – could that have accounted for the disappearance of Lyonesse, the land around St Michael's Mount and many other places which it is claimed have disappeared in the Westcountry, like the area between Whitsand Bay, near Looe, and Rame Head which was said to contain several villages? The answer must be a resounding "yes".

It is quite possible for a geological fault to cause the land to sink slowly at first and then suddenly as the fault-line slips – and the rocks at Land's End do exhibit quick fracture lines, as if the land suddenly broke away. Gradual erosion would have left a shallow sloping landscape. Added evidence that there was land further out to sea at one time is the recent find of petrified tree stumps in Mount's Bay – and a portion of a petrified tree from the bay is on display in Penzance Museum.